AD Architectural Design

Extreme Sites

Guest-edited by Deborah Gans and Claire Weisz

WILEY-ACADEMY

Architectural Design

Vol 74 No 2 March/April 2004

ISBN 0-470-86709-4
Profile No 168

Editorial Offices
International House
Ealing Broadway Centre
London W5 5DB
T: +44 (0)20 8326 3800
F: +44 (0)20 8326 3801
E: architecturaldesign@wiley.co.uk

Editor
Helen Castle
Production
Mariangela Palazzi-Williams

Art Director
Christian Küsters ↳ CHK Design
Designer
Scott Bradley ↳ CHK Design
**Project Coordinator
and Picture Editor**
Caroline Ellerby

Advertisement Sales
01243 843272

Editorial Board
Denise Bratton, Adriaan Beukers,
André Chaszar, Peter Cook,
Max Fordham, Massimiliano
Fuksas, Edwin Heathcote,
Anthony Hunt, Charles Jencks,
Jan Kaplicky, Robert Maxwell,
Jayne Merkel, Monica Pidgeon,
Antoine Predock, Leon van Schaik

Contributing Editors
André Chaszar
Craig Kellogg
Jeremy Melvin
Jayne Merkel

Abbreviated positions:
b=bottom, c=centre, l=left, r=right

Cover: © PhotoDisk, inc;

AD
p 5 © Digital Vision; p 6 © PhotoDisk, inc; pp 7 & 8(t) © Robert Liberty; pp 8(b) & 9 © Prendergast & Associates; pp 10(tl) & 11 © Portland Tribune, photos Kyle Green; p 10(br) © Roberty Liberty; pp 13-19 © Renzo Piano Building Workshop, photos: (13r & 19) Stefano Goldberg, (13l) Michel Denancè, (14) Publifoto, (15t) Lingotto, (15b) Enrico Cano, (18t) Banchero, (18b) Shunji Ishida; pp 20 & 24-5 © CoastalPlanners; p 22 courtesy Natural Resources Canada, Geological Survey of Canada, reproduced with permission of the Minister of Public Works and Government Services, Canada, 2004; pp 26-7 © Bridgeman Art Gallery; p 28 © Roni Horn, courtesy Matthew Marks Gallery, New York; p 29 © Philadelphia Museum of Art/CORBIS; pp 30, 32(r) & 33 © Claire Weisz & Mark Yoes; p 31(t) © Hazlitt, Gooden & Fox; p 31(b) © Claes Oldenburg & Coosje van Bruggen; p 32(l) © Richard Rogers Partnership; pp 34-40 courtesy Aga Khan Trust for Culture/Indore Development Authority; pp 41-9 © D Hoffman-Brandt, photos N Miller, D Hoffman-Brandt; pp 54-5 & 58(t) courtesy Ron Shiffman; pp 56(t), 57 & 59(t) courtesy Joan Byron; p 56(b) © Projekt Ruhr GmbH, Essen; pp 58(b), 59(c & b) & 60 © Peter Zlonicky; p 61 courtesy of the artist & Galerie Lelong, New York; pp 62-3 © Andy Goldsworthy; pp 64-8 © Michael Sorkin; p 66(tl) coutesy Michael Sorkin; pp 69-76 © The Beracha Foundation; pp 77, 79(bl & r) & 80-81 © Ramón Paolini; p 78(l) © Carlos Brillembourg; pp 78(r) & 79(tr) © Cartografia Nacional de Venezuela; pp 82-6 © Gans & Jelacic; pp 87 & 89 © D Hoffman-Brandt; p 88 © Deborah Gans; pp 90 & 92(r) © Max Dupain; p 91 © DACS 2004; p 92(l) © The artist courtesy of the Aboriginal Artists Agency, Sydney; p 93 (l) © Reg Morrison/Auscape; pp 93(tr), 94(l) & 95(l) courtesy Mitchell Library, State Library of New South Wales; p 93 (br) © Anthony Browell; p 94(r) © Reiner Blunck; p 96(r) © NASA.

AD+
pp 97-8 © Jeff Goldberg/Esto; p 101 © Peter Cook/VIEW; pp 102-05 © Eric Parry Architects; pp 110-13 & 115-16 © Hélène Binet; p 114 © David Grandorge; p 117 © Sergison Bates Architects; p 120 © The Architects Journal; pp 122-25 © Anamorphosis Architects.

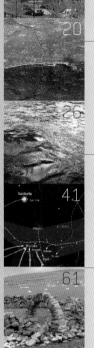

Subscription Offices UK
John Wiley & Sons Ltd.
Journals Administration Department
1 Oldlands Way, Bognor Regis
West Sussex, PO22 9SA
T: +44 (0)1243 843272
F: +44 (0)1243 843232
E: cs-journals@wiley.co.uk

Annual Subscription Rates 2003
Institutional Rate: UK £160
Personal Rate: UK £99
Student Rate: UK £70
Institutional Rate: US $240
Personal Rate: US $150
Student Rate: US $105

AD is published bi-monthly.
Prices are for six issues and include postage and handling charges. Periodicals postage paid at Jamaica, NY 11431. Air freight and mailing in the USA by Publications Expediting Services Inc, 200 Meacham Avenue, Elmont, NY 11003

Single Issues UK: £22.50
Single Issues outside UK: US $45.00
Details of postage and packing charges available on request

Postmaster
Send address changes to AD Publications Expediting Services, 200 Meacham Avenue, Elmont, NY 11003

Printed in Italy by Conti Tipocolor.
All prices are subject to change without notice. [ISSN: 0003-8504]

Extreme Sites
Guest-edited by Deborah Gans and Claire Weisz

ΛD

Extreme Sites extrapolates for us a fresh view. Honing in as if by satellite, it brings us into contact with brownfield sites that span the world from the relative comfort of Portland, Oregon, and Genoa, northern Italy, to the slum conditions of Caracas and the refugee camps of Africa. The notion of site is not bound by the terra firma – land, ocean, natural drainage paths and rivers alike all come under scrutiny. Through the specifics and the contrasts of the issue's geographically disparate contributions, Deborah Gans and Claire Weisz artfully build up what they refer to as the 'unprecedented weaving together of the naturalist and urbanist'. For the emphasis of this title, which deals with the 'extreme' – large tracts of land that are explicitly other, contaminated and generally fouled up by humankind – is very much one that relies on a holistic understanding of the environment and a basic acknowledgement of innate connections. This presents an ideal but is also wholly pragmatic, as so clearly summed up by Himanshu Parikh's remark in his article on slum networking along the Indore River: 'the brownfield site is continuous with the fabric of the city, as the city is likewise continuous with the slum'. Neither natural or urban systems can ever afford to be wholly exclusive, whatever the given definition of nature or the city. △

A brownfield is a contaminated site, ground rendered unfit for human occupation through human activity. Its companion term, greenfield, refers to a yet undeveloped ground, implying that the very act of development might render it, to some degree, brown. While not much more than ten years old, these neologisms redress the still unmet challenges of a first wave of calls for environmental and urban reclamation, in books like Rachel Carson's *Silent Spring* and Jane Jacob's *The Rise and Fall of Great American Cities*. They arrived on a more global scene and have a global usage, a new Esperanto of ecology and politics that recognises the extent and interconnectedness of our interference with nature's systems. They reshape our understanding of site through their binding of human and natural factors together. We have organised the issue according to that binding of place and action: the mine, the port, the river bank, the coastal site, the agricultural field, the landfill, the dam and the camp site. They are extreme in their circumstances because they are simultaneously damaged yet at the centres of human concern, theatres of our often cyclical will to plan, build, grow, prosper and abandon.

A brownfield is a latent condition, as yet unreclaimed, unbuilt. Too often the approach to its remediation is driven by economics and litigation rather than by a conceptual framework of landscape, urbanism and culture. The coincidence of development pressures and new environmental technologies has resulted in a growth industry of brownfield reclamation, the parameters of which arise from outside the language of design and the impulses of planning. The projects and essays in this issue set out a framework of landscape, architecture, urbanism, anthropology and art for understanding brownfields and their subsequent reclamation as large-scale human interventions in the environment. Portland serves as a model project of negotiation between the demands of ecology and of development in terms of the specific identity of a site. Renzo Piano and Glenn Murcutt take the extreme positions, the former defining brownfield as simply the historical condition and greenfield as the total absence of meaning, while the latter considers even the European idea of property as an act of contamination. The mines of Emscher Park and of Sorkin's Leipzig are 'absences' that become not only active 'presences' but also redeemers of urbanity as they become the focus for acts of civic will. The stories of Indore, Caracas and London challenge the characterisation of the brownfields as 'other' and discuss them rather as part of the continuity of a city's life and landscape. In the refuse dump of Israel, the flood plain of northern Syria and the refugee camp of eastern Africa the brownfield condition is the catalyst for imagining new patterns of culture and settlement. We see in all these projects the opportunity for an unprecedented weaving together of the naturalist and urbanist. Δ

Previous Page and below
Two examples of brownfield where the landscape is dominated by smokestacks and by a massive strip mine.

Portland Oregon:
The New Model of Urban Redevelopment

The reclamation of the Portland waterfront, as described by **Matthew Jelacic** after his recent site visit there as Loeb Fellow, contains a history of the ecological movement in the US as well as an admirable scenario for brownfield development. Concern with the contaminated condition of the site dates back to the early 1970s, just a decade after Rachel Carson's *Silent Spring*. A regional viewpoint that allowed natural boundaries to supersede local political ones emerged several years later. The culture that developed from these early forays into environmental practice spawned the River District Plan, specifically the bold restriction of sprawl and the provision of housing for all income levels. In this, Portland is exemplary, as its placement as the first project in this issue attests. Yet the mandate of the essays that follow is to test its limits and question its parameters, as well as celebrate and encourage the proliferation of similar accomplishments.

A combination of factors contributed to the dramatic turnaround of this dying inner-city industrial wasteland into a vibrant urban residential and commercial district, but perhaps none is as important as the simple economic relationship of supply and demand.

Previous page
The commercial success of Portland's River District is the result of a comprehensive planning process that included advanced remediation techniques, renovation and new construction, and the first tram system in the US for over 50 years.

Above
New construction and renovation began quickly after remediation programmes made land available.

Right
Adjacency to the Willamette River, its extensive system of public waterfront parks and public transport were critical components for the success of the River District's redevelopment, but also required sensitive remediation solutions.

Portland, Oregon became a mecca for urban planners in 1973 when a political moderate, Republican governor Tom McCall, signed into law a bipartisan bill calling for planning to take place at state level. As an outgrowth of this law, Portland's regional government, the Metro Council, was created in 1979, and is responsible for a range of projects, none more important or effective than its Urban Growth Boundary. This limit on suburban sprawl has fostered a range of planning initiatives including a comprehensive transit system, a ground-breaking urban wildlife and park system, and a brownfield redevelopment project in the heart of the city that is an unparalleled economic and community success.

The River District and adjacent Pearl District, named after a local artist, are a model of redevelopment. Beginning in the early 1980s, a large 70-acre industrial area began to entrance developers. Originally a wetland, filled at the end of the 19th century to make way for development on the Willamette River, the site quickly became an intense industrial zone and a depot for the Burlington Northern & Santa Fe Railway in 1911. This busy railway centre was a repair and fuelling station, cargo transfer point for raw materials extracted from the state's interior, and a manufactured gas plant until the early 1980s.

A combination of factors contributed to the dramatic turnaround of this dying inner-city industrial wasteland into a vibrant urban residential and commercial district, but perhaps none is as important as the simple economic relationship of supply and demand. Governor McCall's campaign to stop 'sagebrush subdivisions, coastal "condomania", and the ravenous rampage of suburbia' required developers to think 'inside the box' for alternatives to traditional American sprawl development.

Starting in the late 1980s, developers began converting the existing warehouses and loft buildings in the Pearl District into residences. Then, after almost 15 years of negotiation between the Metro Council, landowners and developers, which included a 10-year lease of the property by the railway, the demolition of a major highway viaduct that bisected the neighbourhood and the construction of the first tram system in the us for more than 50 years, in 1997 the city adopted plans and guidelines to promote River District redevelopment. Almost immediately new buildings, built in styles that complemented their existing Pearl District neighbours, began to rise on the vacated rail yards.

Although the entire 70-acre industrial area suffered environmental degradation, among the most important concerns for developers, government and citizens was the remediation of the soil and ground water on 26 acres of the site that were damaged by the refuelling and other operations of the railway. Cleanup of the ground water began in 1974 when oily-water discharges into the Willamette River were noticed. However, a complete investigation into the environmental damage to the area was not completed until the 1990s.

In December 2000 the state's Department of Environmental Quality (DEQ) issued a report calling for both soil and ground-water cleanup operations, and identified major contaminants as total petroleum hydrocarbons (TPHS), polynuclear aromatic hydrocarbons (PAHS), volatile organic compounds (VOCs) and lead. The report also outlined a $5.6-million cleanup strategy that included soil removal and 'hard surfaced capping' of the most volatile areas, procedures combined to reduce the contaminants and achieve 'acceptable levels of risk'.

The resurgence of this area has been dramatic. The 1997 guidelines adopted by the city anticipate development of more than 10,000 housing units by 2017. More than 2,500 of these market and rental

Below
Aerial photo of the River District in 1990 showing the Burlington Northern & Santa Fe rail yard and dilapidated industrial buildings at the edge of Portland's Central Business District.

A combination of factors contributed to the dramatic turnaround of this dying inner-city industrial wasteland into a vibrant, urban residential and commercial district, but perhaps none is as important as the simple economic relationship of supply and demand.

Above
New multi-unit housing construction has exploded in the last decade, making the River District a destination for young professionals and families with children.

Right
The River District integrates a range of programmes including commercial space and housing for a broad spectrum of incomes.

housing units will be on the former rail-yard site.
This ambitious plan for new housing construction in
an unfavourable economic environment seemed to
some impossible. However, demand has outstripped
supply dramatically as Portlanders discover the
vibrancy and benefits of urban living. As a result,
more than 1,000 units of housing have already been
built, and more than 2.1 million square feet of mixed-
use space.

The demand for new building sites created by the
limited supply of land available inside the Urban Growth
Boundary gave creative developers and government
officials the incentive to look for unconventional
solutions. Their courageous execution of a visionary,
humanistic downtown master plan that directly
confronted brownfield remediation has made Portland's
River District a model for responsible environmental
stewardship. However, the overwhelmingly successful
transformation of this abandoned industrial area into a
vibrant residential, cultural and commercial new growth
urban area has proven even more important as a
catalyst for long-term environmentally sustainable
planning strategies. ⌂

The 'Brown' and the Contradictory:

An Interview with Renzo Piano

By Renzo Piano's own admission, the historic harbour of his home town of Genoa is a brownfield site. The city's factory since ancient times, its 'modern' 16th-century harbour is built on the site of earlier 14th-century and Roman ports. In conversation with **Amy Lelyveld**, Piano discusses how fecund an influence Genoa and brownfields in general have proved for his practice – 'brown' often providing a rich architectural context and seam of contradiction.

A store-front model shop marks the entrance to the Renzo Piano Building Workshop in the heart of Paris's Marais district. From the street you can watch a truss or an auditorium take physical shape as model builders assemble parts in the space's warm wood glow. The model shop is a good fit in this neighbourhood of refined craft – of expensive handmade shoes, exquisite tea emporia and tasteful antiques. But as a figurehead expression of what the workshop is about, the model shop is also a bit of a tease – a single essence chosen and distilled from the complex mix of reason and passion that feeds a Piano design.

Renzo Piano has called architecture 'a contaminated art on which everything impinges'.[1]

It is in the complex texture of a place, in who and what is and has been there, that he finds the DNA of architecture. In a two-hour interview in Paris this autumn, Piano talked about the earliest sources of his own architectural DNA – his days as a child in Genoa. These experiences, rife with contradiction and complexity, are themes read in his architecture. He characterises the results of architectural process as the 'emergent part of an iceberg'[2] – pure and totemic images that have crystallised out of a process that is anything but pure. Piano is excited by 'the idea that what is supporting architecture is not architecture. It's actually everything that gives the sense for architecture.'[3]

AL We could start talking about the concept of extreme sites. The original idea for the interview – at least the generative idea – was to talk to you about Genoa as an extreme site and your connection to it.

Piano It's quite difficult to talk about that because you know there's an age when you become more aware of how important roots are. When you are young you don't realise. It takes probably 50 years. ... It takes some time to understand how important are the roots and the images that are trapped in your memory from when you are a child.

So I have to say that Genoa has to have an instinctive, irrational, subconscious importance to my kind of imagery. You know, when we designed and built the Centre Pompidou I was 32; it was before I became aware of roots. When people were talking to me about its imagery of the ship in the city I was a bit surprised. But probably it was quite true. Somebody said that when you are 10 years old you have already got the essentials; except that you spend the rest of your life forgetting that essential. And then there's a moment when you start to go back.

Certainly it's quite true that in my imagery the harbour of Genoa and the ships and the cranes are very important. ... It is the most ephemeral – even precarious – kind of *paysage* you can think about. It's precarious because it doesn't stop to change. All the time. The ships are like big immense buildings but they move away. The same place, next morning, is completely different. But it's also precarious because everything is floating and moving. Nothing stands. When I was a little child the best thing my father could do was take me on a Sunday

or a Saturday to the harbour. The harbour was, at that time – especially when you had cranes lifting things – flying, an incredible image. When I was a child the way they were loading and unloading cars was by putting nets around the cars and lifting them.

... And the water of course is another element of instability. The water reflects the sky. So when the sky is blue the water is different from when the sky is full of clouds. It's a kind of ever-changing world in every sense. On top of that the psychological and social life there is completely different. The anthropology of the harbour is completely different. It's full of different people coming from everywhere in the world. Talking different languages. It's like a Babylonia. A modern Babylonia. Where everything is new. And everything has a smell – a different one – coming from far away. The harbour is like a movie where, when you are a child, you can imagine your life projected to different worlds. The harbour is a place where you can dream for ever. You can dream about this or those ships, or those people coming, and their black faces, or yellow faces or long eyes, from another world. ... This harbour of childhood does mean something; because you grow up in a kind of a world where your expectation of discovering the rest of the world is built up in your day-by-day life.

AL There's everything you talk about, the ephemeral nature of the harbour. But there's also the intense stability of the city facing the harbour.

Piano Those are the two extremes. As much as the harbour is unstable, precarious ... so the city's about duration, stability. It's made of stone. Paul Valéry, the French poet, said a nice thing. He said that Genoa is like a quarry of Ardoise ... slate ... It's dense. It's

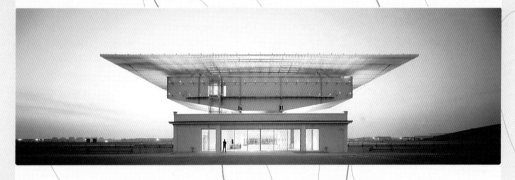

like a kasbah. Genoa, instead of being made
like other cities by making streets and making
buildings by the streets, was made by
starting from the solid volume and then
cutting streets. You understand when you live
in Genoa why it was like that. One reason is
practical because, of course, Genoa is a city
without land. Genoa is compressed between
the mountain and the sea. ... But the other
reason relates to when you have travelled
from far away and you just leave the ship and
your desire is to retreat inside. On a windy
day in Genoa, if you live in the centre of town,
you realise why the city is so compressed.
It was for a sense of protection, almost like a
mantle. So the harbour is a place of adventure
and discovery and the city is the place of
protection and introspection. It's not just
about duration and precariousness; it's also
about introversion and extroversion. In that
sense Genoa is a place of extremes. ... So the

character, it's difficult to say, the character of the
people of Genoa was made by the city or the city
was made by them.

The first thing I inherited from Genoa is probably its
character. The desire for solace, and for a bit of time
for just living with the dust coming down around you.
And at the same time the desire to discover and to go
out. But the other thing inherited is the image. When
you are a child you create an image in your eye – like
a postcard from the past ...
AL Are those images of the precarious harbour rather
than of the solid buildings in a severe topography?
Piano Of the harbour, lightness. I never understood
where my passion for lightness comes from. Probably
I am postrationalising by saying that it's because
my father was a builder. I found that fighting gravity,
looking for lightness, was a kind of challenge against
weight. But all this is very rational. In the end probably,
all this is very much the image coming from the
postcard. I don't want to spend the evening in self-
analysis but in some way there is that sense ...

15

'The Potsdamer Platz was in some ways a black hole. No doubt about it. But not industrial. It was made by the Cold War.'

Above and right
From 1992 to 2000 Renzo Piano built eight buildings for the Daimler-Chrysler project in what had been the no-man's-land between East and West Germany. Because of the site's high water-table and environmental concerns relating to site drainage, divers set the buildings' foundations. The views shown are of this difficult construction site.

Above
This pedestrian bridge
(1999–) in Sarajevo connects
residential areas to future
museums and university
buildings lying beyond the
infamous 'Zmaja od Bosne' –
the wartime Sniper's Alley –
that runs parallel to the river.

AL We talked about the extremes of Genoa. But would you characterise it as a brownfield site?
Piano The harbour of Genoa is a brownfield. It's been a brownfield from the 14th century. Even before. When we worked there we found a Roman piece of harbour ... But the modern harbour – the one that saw Christopher Columbus going somewhere, the 16th-century one – is a harbour that has been the factory of Genoa for a long time. ... It is a brownfield with all the characteristics of brownfields, except that it is historical. Normally the ones that we call brownfields are the ones made by rail tracks and by factories. Lingotto was built in 1925 with all the normal industrialisation of that period. Its rail tracks are from the 19th century. And there are also very funny brownfields like the Berlin Wall, a political thing, made by the Cold War.
AL And your Potsdamer Platz project?
Piano The Potsdamer Platz was in some ways a black hole. No doubt about it. But not industrial. It was made by the Cold War. Not even the war. Because the wall was built in 1962 not 1945. So in some way between 1962 and 1989 when the wall went down, that piece of the city in the centre of Berlin was actually like a brownfield. So the brownfield concept mainly comes from these sources: industrialisation, rail track and a very special case like Berlin. But in a harbour city it also comes from the harbour, which was

for such a long time the factory of the city. That factory is full of memories, full of ghosts in some cases. A harbour that is four centuries old has so many things. ... It's probably the oldest brownfield we have worked on.
We have done a lot of work on brownfields, from the Schlumberger factory to the new extension of Columbia University in Harlem. On the Harlem site you can still find the Studebaker factory, a very old milk factory, and the first storage for pianos in New York. ... Even the little Morgan Library job is about these complexities. There are buildings from 1906, 1926 and 1950. And we are now digging down. It's a funny thing, like an iceberg that goes down. And we put all the vaults underneath. It's almost always about mixing memory. ... It's quite rare to have an empty field.
AL Would you say that you have a different attitude towards developing those sites from any others?
Piano It's less frightening. In some ways the white paper is frightening. In some ways the most frightening scheme I remember was the Kansai airport. The first time I went there we asked the Japanese to take us on the site. And there is no site. It was water. Since it was water we went out in a boat. And we spent one day there. There was nothing. Nothing.
AL Even for someone brought up on the water?
Piano Even so. It's frightening because you have nothing, nothing, nothing. Nothing to grab on to. You are shipwrecked. So in the end, the truth is that no, there is no difference between brownfields and other sites. You have the same attitude, this mix of desire to invent, to find things and also to grab on to things. But it is a bit

This page
In Genoa a 1960s-era highway works as a dividing line between stability and instability, between the promises of the harbour and the deep culture of the town. In this context Piano's Bigo project – a crane designed for the city's 1992 Columbus International Exposition – becomes a monument for instability. It carries a lift and offers a panoramic overview of the city that has always looked down on the sea.

easier when you are working in an existing field, because then the city's there ... it's providing you with the rules, with a kind of discipline.

AL I guess if you believe in architecture as a kind of transformation – even redemption ...

Piano Architecture in the city is about mutation. ... In fact, the word we are using today more and more when we talk about Harlem is mutation. It's using those existing things as an element of transformation.

And this is the big debate going on today in Europe: peripheries. The peripheries of cities are the cities that will be. For the moment they are not cities. The peripheries are impossible places to be. But in some way – through the mutation – they may become happy places to be and to stay.

... This is our guilt. In the 1960s and 1970s the big guilt saved historical centres. Now it focuses on peripheries. In some ways the guilt has expanded because historical centres are more genuine, more beautiful and the periphery ugly, terrible. But in some way it's absolutely clear that today the key words are mutation and transformation and periphery in European places.

Urbanity's a very funny thing. It's not just made by stones and by buildings but by people and activities. The first element of urbanity is mix of function. This is why architecture is so much mixed with sociology and anthropology and all that. ... There is a human side.

It is not a desert. These are traces that you can follow. If you have what they call the social angst – the desire to understand, a kind of ethic in your job (I don't want to be moralistic) then it helps a lot.

AL And it seems to me that you do. It runs through your work and your projects with UNESCO.

Piano I am actually a goodwill ambassador for UNESCO in charge of a few projects. There is one about the periphery of Sarajevo and how we can link things together.

Honestly, architecture is a very dangerous profession where you can easily fall into the trap of academy. You become self-referential – especially if you are a success. You develop a kind of style and you get trapped in the style. You get trapped in what everybody expects from you. Like a rubber stamp – a Versace stamp or Christian Dior or whatever. The only way to escape is to give priority to the emergent part of the iceberg, everything that is not really visible but that makes architecture. That is topography. That is geography. It's history. It's society. It's anthropology. It's all those things. ... What is supporting architecture is not architecture. It's actually everything that gives the sense for architecture.

To come back to your question, because the brownfield is brown it is the opposite of being immaculate and pure, that is without any inspiration. It is full of inspiration. It's full of smell. And texture. The opposite is just a kind of pure abstraction. Although, there's always a point in architecture when everything comes down to the object. And you have to do it and you have to do it well.

AL There's a duality in your work – actually a number of them: between politics and craft, programme and technology, lightness and ...

Piano I believe in contradiction. I really believe that we should not even try to sort out those contradictions. Architecture is about contradictions. It is about stability and instability. It is about memories and invention. It's a mix. Of course you are for memory and you are for invention. There is another famous contradiction between discipline and freedom. But are you so silly to say that you prefer freedom over discipline? It's always about history and future. Trying to solve those contradictions you become stupid. Life is complicated. And architecture is even more complicated because it mirrors life. ... And this tension is aesthetical – it's formal in some way. I love that [indicating a design for a moving mast at the top of his New York Times Building]. It's almost like a movement between two worlds, the world of massive and the world of lightness, the world of opacity and the world of transparency. ... All those elements of contradiction and duality are the ones that give you complexity ...

We just got back from New York and Dallas and everywhere else. And here, now we stay quiet. You need calm to react. You need time to metabolise. The real risk in our world is to have no information. It's a world where people know more and more and yet they understand less and less. In some way our research is just this, to give the time to dream about something. To think. To understand. You touch it. You feel it. It's about all those things coming together. There are many stupid people who believe research is about technology. It is not true. It's like saying for a good artist there's a difference in the touch, between a piece of marble and the idea. Constantin Brancusi spent a month cutting a piece of stone, or polishing it. I can't separate the technique from the idea. In the time you do something you think: you think about flowers; you think about leaves; you think about the final thing; you think about lightness. You combine the practical and material. Architecture is very much materialistic. But at the same time it is idealistic. ⌂

Above
'Of the harbour, lightness. I never understood where my passion for lightness comes from. Probably I am post-rationalising by saying that it's because my father was a builder. I found that fighting gravity, looking for lightness, was a kind of challenge against weight.' To date, Renzo Piano has built four yachts. The *Kirribilli*, shown here, is the latest.

Notes
1 Peter Buchanan, *Renzo Piano Building Workshop, Complete Works Volume I*, Phaidon (London), 1993, pp 11–12.
2 This interview.
3 This interview.
4 Renzo Piano, *Logbook*, Monacelli Press (New York), 1997, p 104.

No Here There:
Designing No Place

In the words of the architect/biologist team **Ted Cavanagh and Alison Evans**, 'the territorial waters of most countries are sites of increasing and conflicting human use. Resource extraction, touristic gentrification and increasing privatisation are gradually modifying the dynamic ecology and natural resilience of the ocean and coastal waters. Over-fishing and habitat destruction are endangering many species that currently sustain the world's coastal population. The ocean receives the "downstream" impact of land use – often the result of tiny individual decisions that accumulate insidiously – known as non-point-source pollution. Our continued practice of the hardening of our land and coasts is just one instance of our inability to adapt to environmental forces. In short, the coastal zone is a site of increasing jeopardy.' The ways in which ecological problems goad us into redefining the shape of our environment and of space itself are dramatically presented in this case study of the larger North American eastern seaboard.

'In the United States there is more space where nobody is than where anybody is. This is what makes America what it is.' — Gertrude Stein[1]

Question

On land we can visualise the spatial impressions of culture and nature. Normally, these visualisations are represented in map and plan. We design with them, integrate their processes with some degree of predictability and negotiate the results publicly. On water, this is not yet possible.

Imagine mirroring land patterns on lakes, rivers and oceans. Perhaps some version of Chicago's mirror image already exists in Lake Michigan. Imagine a 'town' meeting for a specific ocean locality. Who is invited to the meeting, who do they represent and what is their capacity for argument and action? Can we re-create this effective cultural institution for a place with apparently no 'here' there? Who listens? How do we portray, depict and model the place and its future? The ocean is becoming defined, limited and patterned by ownership. Rights of use and natural reserves are appearing on our maps. How can architecture become involved in the extensive design projects already organising human activity offshore?

Situation

There is a lack of spatial discernment and cultural understanding of our oceans. This is hardly surprising since, as a society, we generally consider the ocean as 'empty' with no, or few, spatial characteristics and no evident cultural ramification. This lack of cultural import is a misconstrual – in fact, the ocean is home to diverse and extensive human activity which is necessarily both social and cultural. Activity evident on recent maps of the 'offshore' depicts the anthropographic ocean as a complex, managed, organised space. The maps show sophisticated representations of natural phenomena and a wide range of human occupation such as traffic corridors, telecommunications infrastructure, property and mineral rights lease lines, fishing zones, conservation 'parks' and tourism trails. With the level of activity offshore it becomes advantageous to add social and cultural organisational practices – perhaps the techniques and skills of design – to current legal, scientific and managerial methods of organising ocean space.

In our work we search for strategies that promote diversity, such as the diversity of human use and the

Opposite
Land and water
Chicago's invisible city, its mirror image, may already exist in Lake Michigan. The top half of the collage depicts the land-based activity, its traces and its patterns, framed by a sample of aerial photography. Water-based activity saturates the bottom half, organised in corridors, lanes, zones, habitats and patterns, some on the surface, some on the bottom, and many in the water column between. Nevertheless, it is represented as 'empty' or a mere reflection of Chicago land patterns. The image is framed by underwater laser bathymetry mapping.

Above
Mapping
Louisbourg, Nova Scotia. The map combines two forms of remote imaging – aerial photography and underwater laser bathymetry. Notice the unresolved shallow water areas between the two forms of imaging. The resolution of the underwater mapping exceeds standard aerial photography.

ignorance of the pervasive cultural land-use patterns of suburb and extra-urban settlement, feeling it unworthy of basic architectural consideration. Like the suburb and the countryside, the ocean is occupied with a wide range of spatial practices. The processes of suburbanisation, community improvement and harmonisation with nature have been part of regional and urban design since the 19th century. Architects are educated in the history of their discipline – a disciplinary memory that includes instances of effective strategies, recurring mistakes and unexpected consequences of apparently simple land-use controls (for example, zoning, easements, designation, public process). Ocean management would benefit from an understanding of this historical experience and this concept of unexpected (unintended) consequences.

Past experiences on land can be translated, either knowingly or unknowingly, into ocean space. These same processes can be easily translated across history or space to a set of equivalent practices emerging in the coastal zone: suburban sprawl continues, transformed, as the population disperses to the small coastal towns of our region; work with inner-city neighbourhoods is hauntingly similar to attempts being made to reinforce the traditions of fishing and seafaring communities; and a new national park system is being defined offshore. And so we replicate the previous spatial practices of our society. We do so despite the difficulties and experience we have had on the land. We repeat the same disputes between farmers, ranchers and wildlife hunters – but now on the ocean. We understand the national parks system (and thus marine-protected areas) and the conflict between public access and protected environments. For better and for worse we are extending land practices on to the ocean – a space of three dimensions.

Practice
Our practice works with these issues in various ways. No single type of project can answer a question this large, and our work is at times conceptual and at others pragmatic. We have worked with community groups and government officials to frame a response. Design helps bring perspective to projects of science and environmental management. In the 'coastline' and 'zoning' examples that follow, we initiated projects that filled a gap in current thinking and practice, albeit along the coast rather than on the ocean; each project involved theory, creative activity, interacting with science and initiating community dialogue.

As indicated by the phrase 'no here there', the situation offers and demands a reconsideration of theoretical conventions such as 'place'. These translations of basic conceptions are a creative act based in historical consciousness that seems embedded in architectural practice. We reconsider

diversity of habitat, and this can be judged according to the indicators of community health – individual, social, economic and ecological. We think that there is something of this in the everyday working vernacular of our region – a tradition of design knowledge apparent as a historical axis within local creative acts. A working vernacular that is distinct from the domestic vernacular of the suburb and the tourist. Creative acts that become a set of 'rolling' solutions, constantly adjusted to meet new circumstances at least partially caused by the previous solutions. An innovative social learning system that lives with turbulent situations where there are unexpected consequences of human actions. This attitude is fundamental to many of the successful projects in our region – projects that reconstruct social values focused around particular issues in a proactive way.

History
The perception of the emptiness of ocean space is not new – architects have thought space to be vacant before. In the first half of the 20th century the profession as a whole affected

many simple spatial qualities such as place, coastline, zoning and representation subject to the recurring desire of structuralist patterning. So while much of our work involves community-based design, some of it is initiated by ourselves as a creative response to a situation.

Coastline Project

A coastline defies the assumptions and preconceptions of linear geometry. As observed by the British mathematician Lewis Richardson, a small segment of a coast is really infinitely long and complex, depending on the scale of observation. A coastline is far-reaching, a shared line of inhabitation that physically extends from the local to a global community. The coastline extends through rivers and estuaries. Its cultural, historic and ecological linkages are deeply embedded regardless of the imposed boundaries of a land-centred state. The coastline is a complex sequence of folds – geographical relationships only sensible to coastal communities.

'Coastline' is a historical term delineating a clear boundary between land and sea. Gradually this term is becoming anachronistic in favour of 'coastal zone'. The switch from a one- to a two-dimensional concept, from 'line' to 'zone', associates the coast with two-dimensional spatial practices: cartography, land-use zoning, habitat mapping and demographic pattern. This ignores the dimensions of height/depth and that of time, essential to any study of complex systems, and even linear conceptions deserve continued consideration.

The project starts with a series of reconnaissance and collection journeys staged along various points of the coastline. Forms of mapping and scale are determined by a sequence of one-hour journeys using a variety of scales of mobility. These journeys examine the coastal points from the global to the microscopic. We create an unfolded and layered visualisation of the spatial complexity of a coastal region using simultaneous representational scales. The content is both scientific and cultural in nature, yet does not privilege one over the other.

We explore the 'space' of scientific visualisation and fuse it with cultural, historical and experiential representation. All the phenomena explored – historical, economic, geological, ecological and biological – have relative scales of representation which, as they become more focused and at a smaller scale, find themselves in the phenomenological realm of the tactile lived world. The form and scale of each journey is a one-hour time line determined by a gradually collapsing scale of movement by satellite, plane, car/power boat, bicycle/kayak and on foot.

The graphic premise begins with the geographic standards of description. We 'unfold' the coastline of Nova Scotia as an ordering system and datum for visually understanding the network of coastal communities. The unfolding of the coastline also maps the coast at a multitude of scales based on the premise that coastlines are potentially of infinite length. The project is ordered within this linear structure.

The distortion created reveals a tableau of proximity, cultural and historical relationships unavailable in standard geographic representation. There is more spatial logic, for example, to the traditional intercommunity exchange by sea on the Nova Scotia coast than to the recent addition of roads and highways. Moreover, there is perhaps more cultural and historical logic to these coastal settlements based on their topographic origins than to a simple chronology. The challenge, then, is to find a mode of representing (graphically and, by implication, politically) the interrelated nature of coastal communities. A spatial model could form not only the visual forum of the network but may possibly influence the mode of communication as well.

Zoning Project

Zoning has come to mean proscribing or restricting human activity by creating distinct territories with preferred occupancies. It is artificial classification that results in neighbourhoods of uniform density, uniform building form, uniform activity and sometimes uniform character. Usually it creates monocultures and destroys diversity. Unfortunately, zoning seems like a straightforward and practical response to environmental degradation, but it comes with an inherent history and politics. For example, zoning rarely requires social justice or registers qualitative (and therefore often invisible) cultural aspects of society, leading to formulaic repetition of norms based on regulatory minimums.

This is very abstract. To make it clear, a second project uses the visual impact of 'building out' the zoning codes to their maximum planned potential to depict to the communities their current unconscious plan for the future. Of course, as community zoning codes change, these built-out futures change as well. This technique, used successfully in the past, has growing potential with enlarged computing power. In conjunction with community exhibitions and workshops it can return zoning to its historical role as a servant of comprehensive community plans. The current preoccupation with zoning as both ends and means can be mitigated by revised strategies that include new modes of zoning itself: overlay, bonus and performance. People do seem willing to add conservation caveats to their land to meet community-based environmental goals. Shouldn't this be possible on the ocean as well?

Scientists have asked us for a predictive model of coastal development. Often, demographic models are based on population growth projections, projections that did not anticipate the explosive growth in recreational homes on the coast and urban coastal sprawl. An estimate for lower New York State places the rate of urbanisation (hardening of the land in buildings and roads) at eight times population growth. In a manner of speaking, built-out futures are not projections but anticipated facts, design feedback. We draw 'buildings to code' at maximum footprint and

landscape hardness on GIS map layers. This allows scientists to factor-in values of slope, soil permeability and vegetation. New layers can be automatically calculated and generate new maps predicting contours of accumulated non-point-source pollution throughout the watershed and into our estuaries and oceans.

Representation

Increasingly, communities that are outside the urban centres have been left to fend for themselves in addressing economic, ecological and social challenges. In response, communities are 'networking' amongst themselves. While a network may not necessarily improve physical contact between outlying communities, it may help to create a virtual centre with enough critical mass to form a viable communal presence equivalent to those one may find in the larger urban centres. Unfortunately, the maps

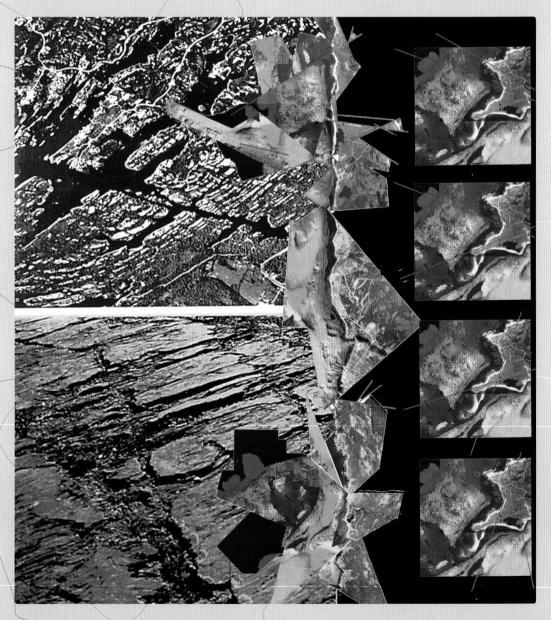

Right
Scale
Coastal Nova Scotia. On the left, notice the similarity of pattern between the 1:10,000 photograph and the one taken at the photographer's feet. These are the two extreme scales of the coastline project. Walking the coastline is depicted by folding out the photo map on page 22; a second series of cuts and unfolding would create an even longer coastline and so on. This collage depicts the fractal nature of the coast. Both concepts – patterns across scales and the fractal nature of the line – are ways of representing scale as it relates to ecological values.

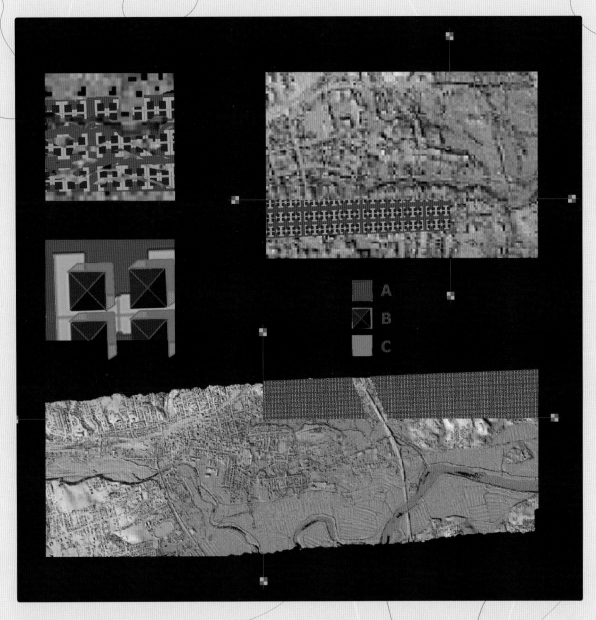

Right
Predicting
Truro, Nova Scotia. Maps and schematics of the town's housing future. These are diagrammatic representations of more elaborated maps that build each zone of the town to its projected asphalt surface (A), maximum allowed footprint (B) and fertilised lawn (C). Scientists use this data to predict impact such as non-point-source pollution. Exhibiting these maps in the community generates discussions about improving plans for the future of the town.

Notes
1 Gertrude Stein, from the poem 'The Geographical History of America' in *The Geographical History of America or the Relation of Human Nature to the Human Mind*, John Hopkins University Press (Baltimore, MD, 1936), 1995.
2 Some of the work is the result of current and earlier collaborations, among them Jennet Bowdridge, Vicki Suijic, Elena Garcia, Craig Brimley, Pat Harrop, Tom Dubicanic and communities, government, scientists and managers throughout the region.

of industry, government and science fail to represent social and cultural practices, and do little to record traditional or local occupation. How can we explain these omissions? It is time to recognise that designers have left coastal and ocean space to be analysed by disciplines with little or no background in representing history, politics and culture.

Gradually, ocean uses, settlement patterns and coastal towns are becoming part of an ever-increasing managerial realm. The net effect is to exclude structures of community initiative and of local governance despite laudable and progressive goals of inclusion. Design professionals can contribute to planning coastal and ocean areas by adding the analytical and synthetic techniques native to their discipline, by including social and cultural issues in a broad,

practice-based, critical framework and by voicing their independent and legally mandated concern for the public good.

Overall there is a significant invasion of global interest on a previously local geography. Part of the goal of our project is to demonstrate, through the introduction of architecture, the significance of social and spatial history and to register the continuity of urban and suburban place-making within contemporary spatial practices of coastal management. We find in the design process the technical, scientific and social possibilities to turn projects that are often fragmentary and unnecessarily repetitive into innovative social learning. There are many questions still to be considered. At their root, however, most questions concern a radical revision of two forms of design and representation – as revised graphics and as democratic constituency.[2] △

The River's View: In the Space of the Thames

Mark Yoes and **Claire Weisz** review what the Thames River has become under the influence of art, commerce and rapid social change. The premonitions of artists like Turner, Canaletto, Claes Oldenburg and Roni Horn illuminate the challenges of creating new meaning for a navigable site that has assumed a huge influence over the modern metropolis. Now, with the dust settling on a succession of shiny bridges and reclaimed industrial monuments, east London and the more environmentally vulnerable parts of the Thames estuary are the new frontier.

The Thames River has built London, and London has built the Thames River. Cities embrace their rivers in a commercial grip. As the mercantile engines shift, the city also changes, and along with it, the river. Inseparably joined by utility and need, rivers and cities construct a larger reality spanning generations of building, history and investment. Architecture and building are the means by which these changes are implemented and reinforced. But like indelible ink, the record of these realities surfaces in the paintings, the writing and the works of artists. London, a locus of contemporary design and building, is now fully transformed by and for a new commercial purpose and has been completely reoriented in great part by opportunity afforded it by the Thames.

So how does a difficult site metamorphose into a something else? The investment in transformation has been substantial. Poverty, filth and industry haven't been eliminated; they've been sent elsewhere. The building continues unabated but the river is quiet. A visitor to the Thames is struck by the lack of commercial shipping. Much of the river traffic is tourist related. It was from such a passenger boat that contemporary artist Roni Horn completed her work 'Still Water'.

An American artist, Roni Horn photographed 50 views of the surface of the Thames River in the Central London area, interspersed with dead-body reports, exhibited first in 1997 and later published in 2000. Each photograph seems to be of a completely different but equally fascinating aqueous world. Sometimes yellow, sometimes verging on a deep marine tone, the waters are just that –

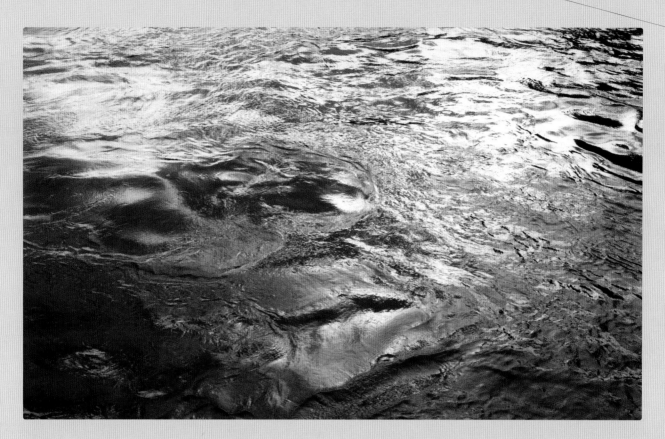

water. Anyone not noting the footnotes recalling the reputation of this body of water and its history of suicides, industry and sewage might savour these views of the water alone. Reading the many footnotes together with the photography causes a similar *frisson* at the new reality of this place. Veering between urban suicidal legends and meditations on the subliminal effect of water, they also capture the effect of this river's changed role and reputation.

> Quote 124: 'This photograph is an image of a moment on the Thames. It is also a moment similar to other moments of moving water and especially moments of rapidly moving water that were hardly visible. But you extrapolate from your experience, you recognize things you've never actually seen – even though you may have watched them as you may have watched this river for hours at a time. But you know it's a river, water moving from here to there. You feel like you've seen it before. But you haven't, what you've actually seen is a slur ...'[1]

The currency of this reductionist view, which focuses on the quality of water itself paired with the notoriety of the Thames as a location for suicide, has a parallel in the new reality of the value of the Thames River, cleaned and cleared for commercial property development.

Water quality has improved dramatically. The murky water in Horn's photographs is the result not of human despoliation but of the fact that the Thames is a tidal estuary with a silty, muddy river bed. The flight of shipping and industry from the banks of the Thames is one of the hallmarks of London's transformation into a postindustrial city. The dislocation caused also created enormous opportunities for the forces of commercial development, Canary Wharf being an obvious example. These 800-foot-tall office towers are the property market's vertical solution to the horizonal fallow expanse of the Isle of Dogs.

But what is it about the river itself that has produced the equation of prosperity through a continual building exposition? Projects like the Thames Flood Barrier that seek to control the extremes of flooding on the river's banks are likely to become more grandiose and comprehensive in the future because of the value of property and the political constituencies that redevelopment will create. Excuses of global warming and the unpredictable surges caused by the warmer Gulf Stream meeting the colder Labrador Current notwithstanding, the barrier is a current urban phenomenon being contemplated for other cities, such as Venice, which need to protect their architectural resources. In short, there was a point at which the Thames changed from being a natural feature that enabled, encouraged and defined human settlement, to a human-mediated and controlled amenity that functions as a light-well for the city, as image and backdrop and as stage for spectacle.

Previous spread
Canaletto's *Westminster Bridge, London, with the Lord Mayors Procession on the Thames*. In the 18th century, Canaletto's idealised view of the Thames was as a setting for spectacle rather than as a working river.

Above
Image on p 37 of Roni Horn's *Another Water (The River Thames, For Example.* Horn's work has influenced, and been influenced by, the ebb and flow of the river's reputation.

In Peter Ackroyd's biography of London the 'fitful and feverish' manner of building in the middle of the 18th century is noted as a pandemic of road building, with development jumping over the Thames into south London as a result.[2] (It is striking to review the press clippings of the 1980s and 1990s where the development of the south bank of the river can be described in the same terms of fever and panic.) Even so, the power of the Thames as a perceptual boundary between north and south persisted despite the surge in the 19th century of bridge building and the resulting integration of north and south into one transportation network. Following Westminster Bridge were Blackfriars, Vauxhall, Waterloo and Southwark, with London Bridge's residential buildings dismantled to maximise the flow of traffic. From an architectural standpoint, it could be said that in addition to creating new connections and areas of density, these bridges opened up the concept of view.

Steeped in the atmosphere of the 18th century, and still creating links with our own contemporary preoccupations, is the work of Canaletto. He had followed his wealthy English clientele to London in the 1740s and was on hand to paint the original Westminster Bridge, newly completed in 1750.

In the views seen by non-Londoners the world over, in collections and digital libraries repeated time and again, is a portrayal of an idealised version of the Thames: pomp and ceremony and blue water. Also present is the concept of the river as a spectacular setting, a divergence from its more pragmatic urgent role as conveyor and conveyance. This artistic view merges in the work of Turner with the power of the sublime and the view of the city as a kind of life force joined by the hip to the river. These are the views imagined by those that ride the London Eye on a foggy day and take the Damien Hirst-designed catamaran from Tate to Tate. Both the London Eye and the catamaran terminal, by the architects David Marks and Julia Barfield, create the kind of urban dynamic and hyperscaled objects that are so successful in the new paradigmatic river front called London.

Charles W Moore was aptly quoted in describing the American Disneyland with the words: 'You have to pay for the public life,' intimating that Europe still had public places without fees. Needless to say, that urban condition has been superseded by the special conditions needed to maximise the view and get the utmost out of the river. The Thames River, which was once the *raison d'être* for London's existence, has been supplanted in practical terms by rail, motor car, air travel and containerised shipping. The trajectory of development of these technologies is related to the transformation

Right
Turner's *The Burning of the Houses of Lords and Commons* (1834) depicts the landscape of the river as binder to the atmosphere of London – apocalyptic and as a vehicle for light.

of a city such as London from a place of production to a place of consumption. What was once a driving factor in the commercial life of the city is now a property selling-point.

Yet the new architecture in the service of urban design plans, such as Richard Rogers Partnership's Tate Bankside Masterplan, does more than simply buttress the premium views and provide new luxury accommodation. Ultimately, the urban strategies of connection and integration of geography are powerfully engaged by the engineering and architectural ingenuity of the new river crossings. Unparalleled, the Millennium Bridge, in particular, uses the section of each bank to insert an instrument of pedestrian accommodation that literally opens up views in a seamless succession of movement, where the water is not only crossed but experienced in a way unlike from any balcony, boat or bridge. Using a striking architectural vocabulary it demonstrates most succinctly that the most powerful engagement with the river is in the crossing of it. The landings on either side seem much more provisional and lacking in conviction than the bridge itself – yet it succeeds. In different ways the floating bridge also sensationalises crossing in its pontoons and light ray, like connections from nowhere to nowhere. Developed by Foster and Partners with sculptor Anthony Caro, this bridge is the only one purely for pedestrian crossing of the Thames.

Pop Art has a central place in any discussion of how cities change so drastically. The sketch produced by Claes Oldenburg in 1967 for one of his colossal monuments for the Thames was probably first seen in an exhibition organised by the Tate in the late 1960s. Updating Canaletto, Oldenburg portrays an ironic spectacle, presaging the Tate Modern's role on the South Bank (the power of the large symbol that goes beyond building was demonstrated somewhat in the summer of 2003 by Paul McCarthy's inflatable in the public plaza here). In reading the image and a sectional sketch, Oldenburg is proposing what looks to be a set of buoyant toilet-cistern floats paired equidistant about the river and Waterloo Bridge. Contemporary London is a geography where the landscape and waterscape of London are spoken of together. To quote Oldenburg, who in hindsight seems more of an urbanist than a Pop artist:

If I am a landscape painter (and my 'monuments' are an excuse for doing landscapes). Then I am a painter of the complete landscape, not only the look of the weather and the lay of the land, etc. but also the emotions of the place (mine and others) this history of the place (some of which I imagine) and what ever else I am aware of in a place. I am unable to leave things out, so I compress and superimpose to get a subject I can handle.[3]

Rather than setting the location of factories, warehouses and transport hubs, the Thames is now an amenity for housing and office development. The Modern Movement's obsession with light and air, coupled with an entrenched romantic notion of the sublime, has been thoroughly internalised into the collective development subconscious (yesterday's romantic and avant-garde notions are the bullet points of today). It is the function of the Thames to provide light and air, views and spectacle for office and luxury housing developments. Canary Wharf has no need to physically engage the river because it captures and frames it, and sells it. And the 'great swathe' of the river no longer isolates the south,

Above
Paul Simonon, former bass player with The Clash, is now known as a painter of the Thames, a career trajectory that resonates oddly with the contemporary development of the river itself.

Right
Claes Oldenburg's *Ball Monument* was a prescient statement of what the Thames would become – a vehicle for art and tourism – with the construction of the Millennium projects.

31

which is newly connected by underground and populated by new offices and loft residences.

The Clash's Paul Simonon is an avid painter of the river. The band's lyrics 'London is burning and I live by the river' reflected the struggle in social values in a time of tumultuous change after the collapse of 1960s optimism and the dismantling of the docklands in the late 1960s and early 1970s. In addition to the Canary Wharf development, the Royal Docks have given way to barrier parks, large-scale housing connected by pedestrian bridges crossing the basins as visual cues to their industrial past. Visionary undertakings such as the Millennium Dome, the mass of which apparently weighs less than the air it contains, are marvels whose technological value is equivalent to the dock and basins of the late 18th century, which in their time were wondrous in their hydraulic mastery and immensity of operation, but whose commercial value has yet to be realised.

The Thames is really no longer a difficult site, because it is no longer contested; it is no longer problematic in the way it once was. It has the opposite connotations that it once did; it is now a desirable feature in any property specification. However, the new problem for the Thames is who will measure benefit from its ongoing redevelopment? Now that it is itself no longer a dirty highway/industrial zone/cesspool, the divide between north and south London is increasingly blurred and the prospect of development to the east inevitable.

Representations of the Thames have alternated between the apocalyptic and the sublime, reflecting the evolution of the river as the main organising principle of London. A bigger Thames still awaits discovery, the one that starts as a spring in the Cotswolds and whose marshes might still be rediscovered for their filtering functionality. Development is veering to the east. The possibility of planning based on the benefits of a river basin may come into play. Experts extolling the benefits of using the River Lea, and planning canal connections as revitalised linkages to the Thames, are seen as sensible when building housing areas on a flood plain. As 'green' technology, barrier parks and wetland and environmental gardens become more convincing as public investments and thus, for architects, the focus for new invention and form, it remains to be seen what role the Thames will play. Claes Oldenburg again has a prescient concept: the river is a metaphor for our own physical frailties and vice versa. Our relationship with the river is empathic rather than dominating, a position we arrive at only after our domination of the river is complete and at the same time unsatisfying.

In London there seemed to be an obsession with water. Body Moisture was agitated to the point where most people had constant colds. Ads showing people blowing their noses filled the newspapers. I proposed a Giant Ear to be placed in the estuary of the Thames. When the tide rose the ear would flood; when the tide went out, the ear would be empty, to be filled and then emptied by the movements of the tide ...[4]

As industry ebbs down river to the sea to depart to other locales both near and very far away, new opportunities for urban growth are created. The development of the whole of southern England is characterised by the tension between the need for more expansion in an already thickly populated region versus the imperative for preserving what greenfield space

Below left
Richard Rogers Partnership's Tate Bankside Masterplan clearly recognises the Tate as a catalyst for development on the postindustrial Thames, and its urban design develops Bankside as a network of architectural events.

Below right
The Millennium Dome is the apotheosis of the Thames estuary as a setting for spectacle in the landscape. Even in its empty state it is still a major tourist attraction.

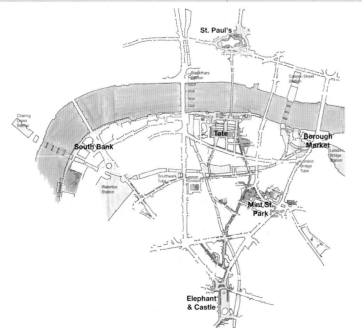

N

LONDON

Hampton Court

Thames
Estuary

Lambeth
Westminster
Hungerford Bridge
Waterloo Bridge
St. Paul's
Millennium
Southwark Bridge
Tower Bridge

Vauxhall Bridge
Oldenburg
London's
Blackfriars
Tate Modern
Globe Theatre
Roger's Bankside Plan
London Bridge

Tate Gallery
Millennium
Eye

West India
Greenwich
Canary Wharf
& Isle of Dogs

Millennium

River

Royal Docks

Thames Flood
Barrier Park

Thames
Gateway

Above
The Thames estuary and its
monuments have become a
new script for London and its
postmillennium identity – an
identity currently being revised
by newer planning for the
Olympic Games and continuing
housing pressures.

Right
View typical of the
postindustrial Thames;
warehouse conversions take
the place of the industrial
waterfront.

Notes
1 Roni Horn, *Another Water
(The River Thames, For
Example)*, Scalo (Zurich), 2000,
p 37.
2 Peter Ackroyd, *London: The
Biography*, Anchor Books (New
York), 2003, pp 510–11.
3 Claes Oldenburg, 'Selections
from Oldenburg's Writings',
Claes Oldenburg (catalogue for
an exhibition organised by the
Museum of Modern Art, New
York, under the auspices of
the International Council of the
Museum, The Tate Gallery,
London, 24 June to 16 August
1970), The Arts Council of
Great Britain (London), p 13.
4 Excerpt from an interview
with Claes Oldenburg
conducted by the poet and
editor Paul Carroll, on the
origins and development of
Oldenburg's 'Proposals for
Monuments and Buildings:
1965–69'. The talk was taped
on 22 August 1968 in the
Artist's Room at Carnegie
House in Chicago. Public
Address, San Diego, California,
28 October 2002.
http://www.publicaddress.us/
images/Oldenburg.pdf
5 Richard Rogers, 'Delivering
the Urban Rennaissance',
Guardian Unlimited, 21 July
2002.

remains. The Thames Gateway master plan represents an attempt to extend the reconceptualisation of the Thames east of Greenwich. What in one sense is negative – the emptying of the commercial–industrial watershed from a property-development perspective – yields a treasure trove of undervalued brownfield sites. The title Thames Gateway implies a conceptual reorientation of the Thames River from a border between north and south to a conduit to a new frontier for development to the east.

Perhaps the most cutting criticism of this strategy of reincarnation is not one of questioning the wisdom of building on a contaminated flood plain but of questioning whether, as Lord Richard Rogers expresses it, 'the Thames Gateway – the largest reservoir of brownfield land in the southeast – is being frittered away for lack of holistic vision and the tools to deliver it'.[5] This challenge, of seeing how this unfettered area of previously low expectations can achieve a density

of use that benefits the greatest number of people rather than exacerbating the East End's severe and long-standing imbalances by escalating property prices and limited development, is now in play.

For better or worse, the Thames Gateway is another instance in a long history of London transcending its accepted limits. As mentioned earlier, until recently the Thames as apocalyptic image was a recurring theme – for example, one need only think of Turner's painting of the burning of the Houses of Parliament in 1834 or of Oskar Kokoschka's view of Westminster, or in more recent cultural history the lyrics of The Clash. The river was viewed this way because it was a site of conflict at the urban scale, and tragedy at the personal scale in the form of suicide. The postmillennium tourist accepts the Thames as monument and spectacle, as a fact of central London. Perhaps the clearest indication that the Thames estuary and what is called the Thames Gateway represent the new frontier is that they are not yet fixed in memory by an artistic vision – by a Canaletto, a Turner or an Oldenburg of our time. ◬

Slum Networking Along the Indore River

For the engineer **Himanshu Parikh**, 'the brownfield site is continuous with the fabric of the city, as the city is likewise continuous with that of the slum'. He presents the isolation of the terms brownfield, infrastructure and slum as a political device that ultimately impedes urban quality. His river-cleaning projects are case studies in a larger search for methodologies akin to holistic treatments of the 'city as patient' rather than surgical interventions at 'the site of disease'. Rivers are powerful examples because, as he notes, natural drainage conditions so often form the initial armature for city plans, and their decay so often reflects the pattern of slum settlement. Parikh's work is contentious, in part because the results can be hard to quantify, and the cause of failure obscured by a tangle of human and physical factors. But his greatest provocation is a complex scenario that shifts the burden of public work to the private citizen and yet simultaneously positions the economically disenfranchised within the mainstream of development. In many ways it is the nature of brownfield, as unstaked, underdeveloped territory, that allows this scenario of a new kind of grass-roots infrastructure to unfold.

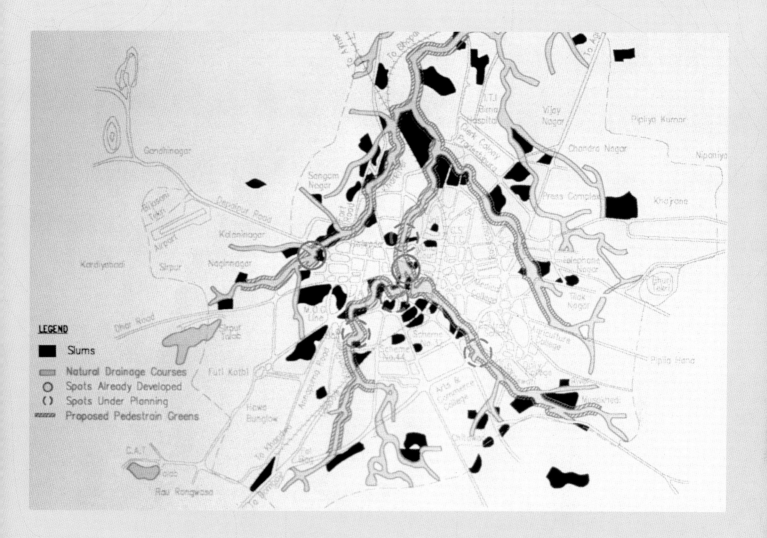

LEGEND
- ■ Slums
- ▭ Natural Drainage Courses
- ○ Spots Already Developed
- ( ) Spots Under Planning
- ▭ Proposed Pedestrain Greens

All cities have strong natural drainage paths. Without these, villages and towns would drown in their own waste long before they ever grew into cities. The paths are nature's own means of disposal and, if properly exploited, also the ideal routes for the man-made urban infrastructure of sewerage, storm drainage, water supply and roads.

Studies of several cities in India, and in other parts of the world, show slums to be consistently located along these natural paths. The environmental skeletons of city greens and water bodies also lie on the same paths. On the other hand, conventional man-made sewerage systems are not necessarily related to natural systems and have their own course, and for this digression they have to pay the high cost of deep excavation, backfilling, manholes and pumping stations. In India, a large part of the population is left out of this artificial network, so that the natural drainage courses become a secondary sewerage system and, simultaneously, the armature for slum growth. Once this connection between slums, urban infrastructure and environment is clearly understood, it is easy to see how slums can be used to transform cities.

Physically, slum networking is an integrated upgrading of the entire city using slums not as isolated islands but an urban net. The slum fabric is seen in the context of the whole city and interventions proposed are mutually beneficial to the slum and its larger context. The objective is not to find solutions unique to the slums but, instead, to explore the commonality between the slums and the better parts of the city and to integrate the two. As slums are not the cause of urban degradation but the consequence of distorted development, the solutions likewise must treat the slums as mere symptoms and use them to work back into the city fabric and to the origins of the problems. The spatial spread of slums over a city together with contiguity between slum settlements gives an opportunity to strengthen the city-level infrastructure networks.

The First Case Study: Indore

Centrally located in India's fertile Malwa Plateau, midway between Delhi and Bombay, Indore is a marketing and distribution centre for cotton, nuts, wheat and other cash crops, as well as an important textile-manufacturing city. Its growth as a business and transport centre has created numerous employment opportunities, resulting in a continuing rural–urban migration of job seekers. Most of these people move into the 183 slums that are scattered throughout the city, many of them on the banks of the Khan and

Saraswati Rivers.[1] As per the 1991 census, the population of Indore city was 1.25 million, out of which slum dwellers accounted for 0.35 million. The Indore sewer system built in 1936 served only 5 per cent of the city's population then. All the sewage and solid waste was discharged into the rivers.

The concept of the networking project was to create an efficient urban infrastructure path for sewage, storm drainage and fresh-water services that follows the natural river course and that would consequently help to upgrade the slums. An extensive physical survey was conducted to plot the city's natural drainage paths to the river, and a socioeconomic survey identified the slum families with the greatest needs. The solution was implemented at two levels. At the city level, a main sewerage artery funded by the Indore Development Authority and Great Britain's Department for International Development was constructed along the river bank at a cost of US$1,800,000.[2]

The added advantage of the coincidence of natural drainage and underdevelopment was that many problems of land acquisition and demolition normally encountered in built-up areas during installation were avoided here. The drainage system was topographically sensitive, with sewerage lines close to the surface so that none was more than 2 metres below the ground and not a single pumping station was required. Within five years, 90 kilometres of sewerage mains were installed giving 50 per cent of the population access to sanitation. Originally the sewage was to be treated using the natural method of 'root-zone treatment by phragmites, but under a new National River Action Plan conventional treatment methods have been effected'.[3] Just by providing the missing links between the slums, it was possible to build up city-level sewerage with the main pipes sized to serve the entire city at costs less than half those for the conventional system proposed by the Public Health Engineering Department.

At the local level, slum dwellers paid for and built their own toilets and connections to the water and sewerage lines at an average cost of 10,000 rupees (US$200) a family. A state government ordinance that gave Indore slum dwellers long-term land leases, effectively legalising their unauthorised colonies, was an incentive for making the sewerage investment. The dwelling plots typically provide space for a one-room house that contains a kitchen, toilet and washroom. Each house was provided with a gulley trap for the removal of waste water and sewage. These gulleys were in turn connected to the main sewerage through covered inspection chambers provided between every six to eight houses.[4]

A comparative study for Indore showed that the cost of house-to-house piped sewerage by networking was about 1,500 rupees per family (US$30) for the lines and 1,000 rupees for off-site collection and treatment. Against this, the cost of a shared United Nations

Development Programme (UNDP) twin-pit latrine, often considered 'appropriate' for developing countries, worked out at about 2,500 rupees per family. Whereas the sewers also take care of the foul waters from kitchens and bathrooms, UNDP latrines do not. The additional advantages of the networked sewers were, firstly, that all the families had individual facilities and, secondly, that other families could also be connected to the same system without recurring off-site costs – that is, the cost per family decreased as the contributing families increased.

The replacement of group latrines at a distance with individual toilets is of great benefit to women, who are at risk of physical attack when bathing. On the physical front in general, women in slums face the worst hardships of environmental and sanitation degradations. Sometimes hours have to be spent just to fetch enough water for the day. Often girls miss school to help with the daily chores of cleaning the house and its unsanitary environs. Women are, therefore, highly motivated to initiate development and play a more mature role in reaching consensus and resolving differences that arise in the community. They also show a greater degree of responsibility in managing money and making repayments. A later networking project in Baroda came to fruition despite a long incubation period of three years simply because of the persistence of the women there to have individual water taps and toilets.

In an extension of the large-scale concept to the microlevel, the roads were coordinated with storm drainage and sewerage to natural gradients in each settlement. In lieu of the conventional practice of raising roads above ground level, causing water to collect on the sides damaging the base and carpet and waterlogging the perimeter, the slum roads were lowered and paved in concrete so that they served as extensions of the natural city-level natural drainage paths right up to the doorsteps. Thus, the community-level sewerage and storm-drainage pipes under the roads were integrated into the macrolevel city service infrastructure with great efficiency and economy. The surface cleanliness of the road margins was achieved with grading and soft landscaping instead of expensive paving.[5] As far as possible, all roads are placed in cut and have positively downward slopes from high points to the watercourses. The surface cleanliness of the margins is achieved with grading and soft landscaping instead of expensive paving.

The improved condition of the flooded and contaminated ground plain, bolstered with the additional installation of streetlights and building of community halls, has led to some dramatic improvements in the quality of the slum dwellers' homes, for once their neighbourhoods were improved they invested in their houses. For example, the facades that line the streets now feature different colours, cornices, railings and other decorations that enhance the city.[6]

The slums naturally benefit from the improved city-level support but the city, too, changes through this symbiotic process. The quantum of physical work in each slum pocket may be small, but the aggregate impact on the slum matrix of 450,000 persons and the city as a whole is high. The polluted rivers are being converted into fresh-

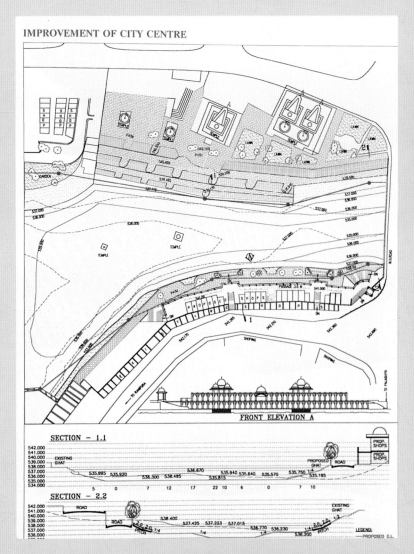

IMPROVEMENT OF CITY CENTRE

FRONT ELEVATION A

SECTION - 1.1

SECTION - 2.2

water lakes in stages, and associated with this the historic riverside structures are being restored and new pedestrian greens formed. A recent study showed that the quality of water in the wells around the areas has improved. Out of the 360 kilometres of roads provided in slums, about 80 kilometres on the slum peripheries were linked up at the city level to reduce the traffic congestion on the existing trunk roads. Similarly, the storm-drainage runs in the slums were placed in such a manner that large areas of the remaining city were also relieved of flooding.

'The pivotal point in the networking project is the *jheel*, the meeting of the Khan and Saraswati rivers, which is also the site of the Krishnapura slum at the centre of Indore. Once full of sewage and garbage, the rivers have been converted into fresh-water lakes and the *jheel* has been transformed into a waterfront area that has revitalised Indore's cultural heritage and the city as a whole. On one bank, 2 kilometres of river front

have been landscaped with curved, paved walkways, flowering plants and shade trees. On the opposite bank, a two-level shopping arcade has been developed.'[7]

In addition to the two levels of physical implementation – the individual and the citywide – there was a third social level of intervention, at the level of community. This included the building of community halls, but more importantly the engagement of the population and the beginnings of community development. A mid-term evaluation of the Indore project showed that 79 neighbourhood committees had already registered under the Societies Registration Act and 70 youth clubs had been formed. Interventions were focused on women and girls who suffer the hardships of slum conditions most keenly and have the greatest potential power to stem the carry-over of the disadvantages from one generation to another. Thus, activities such as mother-and-child care, female literacy, income generation, vocational training and legal literacy assumed special importance. This gender focus was reinforced by the majority representation of women, both in terms of the numbers and also the key positions held in all the projects. In Indore, not only are the majority of members in all the 79 neighbourhood committees women, but women also predominantly hold the positions of chairpersons, secretaries and treasurers.

The soft underbelly of the Indore project is that it is financed from a grant. The replicability value of the work can, therefore, be questioned. Despite all the intentions, the project was eventually delivered by the agency and not executed by the community. Community participation cannot be sustained without commensurate responsibilities, controls and financial commitments of the people. The result of the weakness of community involvement in Indore has been a lack of understanding of the importance of the connectedness of underground sewerage, storm-drainage earth management, landscaping, solid waste and maintenance despite the fact these are closely related to health. Hence, not all families are connected to the system, some studies putting the figure as low as 34 per cent. This has raised the individual home-owner's cost for participation and created an undue burden on the storm-water drains and the street drainage. Many do not have private water supply, some studies showing as few as 20 per cent, and this impacts the service of the toilets. The sweepers of the corporation are uncooperative in terms of the handling of solid waste – sometimes even dumping garbage into the sewer manholes – because they misconceive that an effective system will jeopardise their jobs.

Evolution from Indore to Other Cities
Baroda represents a critical step in the evolution of slum networking. The project in Ramdevnagar, Baroda, moved towards self-sufficiency and also a greater degree of community control over the programme. It was agreed

that 50 per cent of the resources for slum-level works be mobilised internally and that the development, both physical and socio-economic, be undertaken through the community medium with the intermediation of the Baroda Citizen Council, a local NGO. The remaining 50 per cent of the costs came from the Baroda Municipal Corporation and UNICEF, both parties readily partnering the project to test the assumption that the slum dwellers can mobilise huge resources. The status of slum dwellers is that of 'clients'. They not only determine the nature of development but also play an active role in the execution process and the subsequent maintenance of the assets. The role of the external funding agency has shifted from that of a 'benefactor' to a 'catalyst'. Ramdevnagar explodes the myth that the slum dwellers are not willing or able to contribute towards their own development. Because of the close community involvement as a direct partner, Ramdevnagar did not face the same difficulty as in Indore slums with respect to subsequent maintenance.

As the next stage of development, in the Ahmedabad slum-networking project, grant dependency was totally eliminated by inducting the corporate sector of the city in lieu of an aid agency. A pilot slum project was taken up in Ahmedabad as a joint effort between the communities living in the slums, the Ahmedabad Municipal Corporation and Arvind Mills Ltd, a major industrial house of the country. They jointly determined the development and also shared the costs. A local NGO, Saath, together with professionals, were involved as intermediaries. At the slum level the community played a pivotal role in the implementation process. The pilot experiment has now expanded to 26 other slums in the city through various partnerships between the slum dwellers, municipal corporation, microcredit organisations and NGOs within the city-level conceptual framework established for the project.

The work is spreading to other cities in India. In the state of Madhya Pradesh, six cities, including Bhopal, have now been taken up for slum networking to cover the entire slum matrices of these cities. In a more recent development the approach has crossed over to the villages of western India. What was originally conceived for slums has found equal relevance in villages, where infrastructure is very poor but at the same time communities are strong. Of half a million villages in India, none boasts any decent physical infrastructure. Village infrastructure development gives some hope for these villages in the future.

The strategy prescribed above requires sensitive and intense participation by the public in the development process through self-help. The service infrastructure is simplified and modified so that individual services (instead of shared facilities) can be offered to slum and

Right and next page
Lowering the mud roads before paving them was key to upgrading the urban structure in Indore. The lowered streets and pathways create effective natural drainage channels during heavy rainstorms. The quality of life has improved for the city dwellers with the reduction of the effects of dust and mud.

village families at low costs. Thus the communities can participate in the execution of the works as they have the best knowledge of, and sensitivity to, their surrounding environment. At the same time the maintenance burden is reduced and can be shifted from the local government to the individual householders. In a country where settlement development falls strictly within the purview of the state and local governments, this is a very bold transition that will have far-reaching consequences if it comes to fruition.

Under the pressure of rapid urbanisation and a concomitant deterioration in the quality of life of city dwellers, the urban development policy in India has changed significantly, moving towards a position that supports and enables strategies like slum networking. Moving away from being the 'provider' of subsidised housing, the government increasingly sees itself as a 'facilitator' in a much wider sense in its present approach. The emphasis has now shifted to enabling measures such as the improvement of urban infrastructure, development of serviced land, strengthening of local bodies and promotion of new financial institutions and socioeconomic programmes for the urban poor. The policies with regard to slums have also shifted from clearance and rehousing to upgrade and assimilation.

Evidence is emerging that of the four principal areas of intervention for the urban poor – namely health, education, income generation and physical infrastructure – the last is producing the quickest, most tangible and cost-effective turnaround in all indicators of poverty. Where slum infrastructure has been improved, the improvements in the economic and social indicators have followed in periods of just a couple of years. The best attitude for the present development and aid agencies would be to promote actions whereby their existence becomes dispensable because they have a much more businesslike attitude to the development strategies they support. Recent pilot projects have shown that the urban 'poor' can in fact mobilise huge resources and the charitable attitude to them has to be replaced by an approach that increases their self-sufficiency and dignity in such a manner that they do not become a group apart.

Slum networking is the strengthening of existing city-level connections based on the linkages between the slums, natural drainage paths that influence the urban infrastructure and the environmental fabric of the city. Thus slums, instead of being resource-draining liabilities, become opportunities for a quantum change in the infrastructure levels and environmental quality of the city. In a holistic frame, which converges scales, activities, agencies and resources, networking exploits the slum fabric in the context of the total city for sustainable and cost-effective improvement in the quality of life of its people as a whole. △

Notes
1 Cynthia Davidson (ed), *Legacies for the Future: Contemporary Architecture in Islamic Societies*, Thames and Hudson (London), 1998.
2 Priya Florence Shah, 'The magic of slums', *Humanscape*, January 1999, pp 2–3.
3 Davidson, op cit.
4 Ibid.
5 Shah, op cit.
6. Ibid.
7. Davidson, op cit.

WATER LOG

Observations on a Former Flood Plain in Northern Syria

Landscape architect **Denise Hoffman Brandt** examines the legacy of a dam built in a pastoralist region of Syria, and in doing so takes on the question of whether this and other such extreme interventions in the landscape are necessarily bad in themselves. She describes the potential enrichments of ecology and economy. She reveals the complex shifts wrought indirectly on daily habits, on understandings of nature and space, on structures of property and traditions of community. Her essay and project demonstrate the layered, interrelated workings of culture and nature that exceed the reductive scope of terms and tools we currently use for assessing environmental impact.

In May and June 1995, while working on an archaeological excavation in the Syrian Arab Republic, I lived in a village on the former Euphrates flood plain adjacent to Lake Assad. My observation of the physical environment and social conditions within the embayment, an area of flood plain enclosed on three sides by the chalk cliffs of a surrounding plateau, formed the research base for my project to catalyse the region in view of its changed ecology.

Planning is speculation. An orderly process of reason based on incomplete information is applied to complex, continually interactive environmental, social and cultural conditions towards the accomplishment of an objective. The fact that the information on which projections are made is incomplete due to the dynamism of the conditions examined, predicates that the objectives must also, ultimately, be loosely structured and open to divergent possibilities and ramifications within the framework of an overall agenda.

In the case of the embayment, the obvious need for structures to mitigate the extremely degraded environmental conditions of what remains of the Euphrates flood plain adjacent to Lake Assad, for the future of its local communities and the region, was apparent, juxtaposed with an array of historical modes of habitation in the landscape that provided the opportunities for re-establishing the working hydrology of the microwatershed. The foreseeable impacts of planning operations in the area, which address environmental processes, local and regional sociopolitical systems and cultural values, cannot be fixed. Instead, the conditions provoke a challenge to develop a method of planning that can not only absorb but also benefit from variability in degree and means of deployment of the proposed planning structures.

Background

You could not step twice into the same rivers, for other waters are ever flowing on to you.
— Heraclitus of Ephesus

This is no longer true of the Euphrates. In late spring, at the edge of Lake Assad, bleached mud-brick buildings lie scattered along a low ridge. Dry wheat and barley fields run down-slope only to fall over the eroded lake edge. An abandoned home forms a dissolving peninsula in the tidal zone; further out, the top of an ancient city mound projects above the water's surface. Water and land quietly merge here. The sole apparent action is a small tide rippling over rocks reflecting white sky. Looking west, the embayment is revealed as one vast plane tilting towards the lake.

The Euphrates River is being transformed into a chain of lakes. As Turkey and Syria construct dams for large-scale agricultural irrigation projects, flood control and hydroelectricity, the surface and subsurface hydrology of the region have been altered on a monumental scale. The newly accrued large bodies of water begin as lakes in name only, their future uncertain. Lake Assad, a result of the construction of the Tabaqah Dam (completed in 1973), covers 625 square kilometres of former flood plain (50 miles long by 5 miles wide).

The Euphrates flood plain at one time supported plant and wildlife communities that could have dynamically interfaced with the encroaching water to evolve into a self-sustaining riparian landscape: unfortunately at present the heavily degraded steppe provides few resources for such a vast transformation. The gypsum subsoil in many areas makes even irrigated farming difficult. The river no longer seasonally inundates the plain replenishing it with rich, silty topsoil. Half a century of year-round grazing has loosened much of the topsoil that remained, allowing the wind to blow it away in dust devils or the rains to wash it into the lake. As the lake slowly rises, due in part to sedimentation, the surrounding landscape becomes more lunar, characterised by rocky, shallow soil. The exposed hard surface no longer absorbs the seasonal rains, and the former web of perennial stream channels (wadies) has been reduced to three large gullies running down from the cliff face to the lake. Ground-water recharge is diminished as the seasonal rains rush in torrents through the gullies into the ever-rising lake.

Although Lake Assad is increasing in scale it does not teem with aquatic life. The lake has become eutrophic, the oxygen level has dropped and plants, specifically algae, have become the dominant life form. This condition is probably due to a combination of factors: increased use of nitrogen-rich agricultural fertilisers that are washed with sediment into the lake, and the drowning of the flood plain forming an anaerobic river bed comprised of organic material. Under some circumstances eutrophic water can have great biodiversity. In Lake Assad, in the vicinity of the embayment, algae blooms have increased to the detriment of other organisms. Liver flukes, a parasitic microorganism, appear to be the prevailing form of animal life and there is little fishing activity at the lake. Ironically, eutrophic water, unable to sustain animal life, is rich in nutrients and provides a potential alternative resource.

All of the conditions listed here are present to varying degrees when dams are constructed in arid lands. When extreme, some processes such as sedimentation can cause the dam itself to become dysfunctional. In these situations the observation that dams are destructive and not worth the benefits to industrial economies they generally aim to achieve, is often loudly voiced. I would

PLAN AND SECTIONS OF EMBAYMENT EXISTING CONDITIONS

ORIGINAL EUPHRATES CHANNEL	PLATEAU	EXISTING IRRIGATED AREAS
MAJOR SEASONAL STREAM CHANNEL	LIMIT OF LAKE ASSAD	ROAD
MINOR SEASONAL STREAM CHANNEL	SETTLEMENT	HIGH TENSION LINES

Opening page
This view from the plateau
looking north across the
embayment has a settlement
in the foreground. There is
another settlement – barely
visible through the haze in the
upper left.

Above
Map illustrating the
constellation of settlements
within the embayment and the
environmental and
infrastructural networks that
link them.

oppose that point of view; it is not the dam that is inherently ruinous. The negatives of dams can be offset by their positive characteristics, not just to standards of living, but also to their power as monuments to their own dynamic interaction with the landscape. It is when the interaction between the dam and the landscape is unfulfilled, creating a condition of stillness as opposed to movement, stagnation versus liveliness, that dams destroy. In these areas, such as the embayment, the dams do not improve the local standard of living, their transformation of the land is stunted, their ramifications bleak and far-reaching.

The stilling of the flow of water in the region of the embayment is coincident with the state-mandated stilling of a transhumant population. Transhumance is fundamentally a means of

making use of seasonal resources in a sustainable manner, a habit of living based on migration to seasonal grazing grounds. I use the term to make the distinction from nomadic movement, which has a connotation of romantic wandering. Prior to establishment of the nation states there had existed a spatiotemporal continuum in which sedentary, semisedentary and migratory populations coexisted. While investing in regional infrastructure, the leadership of the Syrian Arab Republic has asserted regional political control through settlement of nonsedentary groups. The Welde tribe of Arab Bedouin occupied the territory of the embayment as winter pasture peacefully with the more volatile, nomadic Anazeh tribe as early as the 17th century. The territory was a fluid zone of conflict and accord articulated by seasonal subsistence activities with occasional periods of continuous settlement. Between the Roman period and the 1950s no group inhabited the embayment year-round.

The circumstances of settlement are unclear. Some sources refer to the Bedouin as eager to settle, and others cite failed attempts to do so by various and shifting hegemonies. The village I lived in was comprised of Shafrat (el-Sheferat), a tribe of the large Welde group, who were settled in the 1950s under the authority of the nation state. The neighbouring settlements are generally Welde and Anazeh with a few nonlocal insurgents. In 40 years the settlements have not coalesced into any form of local-scale polity. Authority has limited valence: power is wielded at the scale of extended families and at the scale of the state. The physical form of the settlements registers the structure of the polity. House compounds intersect and nest adjacent to each other with no public domain except for the road cut, a natural stream gully if there is one, and the cemetery.

The basic building unit is the mud-brick or stone wall from which all forms of human and animal habitation, temporary or permanent, open or closed, are constructed. The buildings and associated walls enclose compounds with smaller structures floating inside them. Windows are rarely prominent, and windows on to public space are nonexistent. Everything is constructed from the earth, thus all surfaces have the same tone and texture as the ground leading to the horizon. Inside a warren of house compounds there is often no view to the fields, although when visible the face of the high steppe forms another distant wall. House walls are elevated from

FLUID TERRITORY: EUPHRATES WATERSHED

WELDE MIGRATION   ANAZEH MIGRATION   --- OTHER GROUP MIGRATIONS   RANGE OF KURDS
WINTER PASTURE   SUMMER PASTURE   ▲ TELL / CITY MOUND   AYN / SPRING   BIR / WELL

streets that have been worn deep with tracks, remnants of travel in the winter rains. Despite the monotonous tone, the constant variability in the texture and configuration of the elements creates a subtle but highly modulated environment that seems to be in keeping with the character of its inhabitants. Although technology has transformed daily actions, it has had little impact on the structure of the villages. Private generators have powered the settlements for years, and recently the government connected most of them to the high-tension line that runs across the flood plain. Yet even now, electricity is almost not apparent except for the sound of an occasional radio or television drifting on the wind at night, or the flicker of light in the distance across the plain.

With the political aspects of settlement, it is evident that the most significant factor in the shift from nomadic pastoralism to sedentary pastoral agriculture in the flood plain was the introduction of the diesel pump. The ability to access large amounts of ground water was crucial to the transition to settled agriculture because, without the ability to transfer from summer to winter pasture, surplus grain must be produced over the summer and stored for winter consumption by the herds. Pumps enable irrigation using ground water without the huge labour investment of digging canals for water-wheel or lift irrigation to bring the ground water to the level of the flood plain. Currently, channels supplied by hose from a pump at a well irrigate most gardens and fields. In 1974 there was only one irrigated garden in the village I recently lived in, and the well that supplied the water was 25 metres deep. Today, many of the house compounds have wells, and fields are irrigated with water pumped out from the village. A private pump can replace what had formerly been community-scale water infrastructure. There is little sign of the understanding of surface hydrology that was critical to a group's survival before the availability of large amounts of well water. The seasonal stream channels have become the loci for private dumping of refuse as opposed to a key community resource for water management. Reliance on seasonal water flow has depleted with the number of active wadies. Where a lush flood plain had been fed by a multitude of small stream beds, the embayment's stream channels have become torrents feeding the encroaching lake.

The value of water within the embayment has changed as technology has made what has always been most scarce appear to be abundant.

As part of the irrigation programme that the Syrian Arab Republic instituted when the dam was constructed, pumps were installed and piping laid from the lake to the villages. Lake water is sold by the government and delivered to water towers within the settlements, from which it can be piped out to compounds and fields. Because the water bill had not been paid in six months, lake water was not available in the village in which we were living, therefore the archaeological project imported water from a village adjacent to the lake. Neighbouring women and children would often come to take water from the tank trucked in every few days. Yet, this 'found' water seemed to have no real value as a common resource. Often the tap would be left on and after several weeks a large pool of mud and wild flowers marked the varying location of the water truck. In another instance, the largest area land-holder, a descendant of the family leader charged with distributing the land settlement by the state, flooded his tomato fields in an exceptionally dry year.

The community has become dependent on an ideal of technology – many times throughout the summer we were stopped by farmers and small land-holders asking if we had a machine that would indicate the best place to dig for a well because there was a general concern about the number of local wells that had run dry. The extreme fluctuation of the ground-water table, due to low rates of infiltration and increased levels of discharge, came as a shock to farmers who over the years had slowly severed their habits of living from seasonal impacts. In fact, it was difficult to rationalise the massively visible surface water and the diminishing ground water.

The latent instability of sedentary pastoralism under the conditions in the e mbayment is made apparent by a return to a migratory lifestyle among the local residents. Most families have husbands or sons working in factories in the provincial capital. These men return to villages during the active agricultural seasons to work on the farms and live with their families. The rest of the year they share apartments in an industrial centre.

Additional opportunities for water management are found in Islamic doctrine, which holds the potential to be a unifying structure in the absence of local political and social identity. The Koran adjudicates complex water-rights issues pertinent to arid lands according to rights of usufruct. Rights of usufruct allow the use of another's property providing that property is not altered by such use. This system is effective because it attributes complex rights of ownership and responsibility as it promotes a value system of honourable use through internal controls. Because both surface and ground water defy boundaries, ownership cannot reasonably be fixed. Usufruct allows for sharing water accessible on private land as long as the functional value of the property is not diminished.

Opposite
Map overlaying contemporary and historic modes of occupation across the Euphrates watershed in southern Turkey and northern Syria.

Process

The conditions at Lake Assad provide both a model for analysing the potentially devastating environmental ramifications of dams in arid regions and a conceptual framework for mediation. Agricultural practices associated with settlement have resulted in deforestation, severe soil erosion and watershed degradation, and the conditions are exacerbated by weak local-scale political structures. Simultaneously there exists a local history of adaptation to tenuous environmental conditions through multiple relational behaviour patterns in the landscape, such as varying degrees of sedentary inhabitation and cycles of migration. The acknowledgement of the success of these intrinsic interactions became the basis for the following planning structures.

The approach of my project presents an alternative to planning and urban-design methods that seek to act within complexly interrelated environmental, socio-political and cultural conditions with a singular focus.

The fluid territory of the historic and existing embayment was the subject of my initial mapping. The mapping juxtaposed environmental conditions, infrastructural investment and patterns of habitation, both transient and of duration. The objective was to first establish a complex relational field from which to then isolate environmental, political and cultural factors. These intrinsic factors were then reapplied to become proposed planning structures that could instigate multivalent change. For example, a political factor that interacts with an embedded cultural behaviour that is grounded in an environmental condition operates across many levels of being. These

DISTRIBUTION MAP OF PLANNING AND BUILT STRUCTURES

1 INITIAL AXIS OF LAKE WATER DISPERSAL

2 a WADI EXCAVATION
  b ALGAE DREDGE AND DISPERSAL

3 ELEVATED AQUEDUCT PUMPS WATER UP
  FROM LAKE

4 FIELD OF GARDENS

5 WADI TRENCHES AND MOBILE PUMPS

6 HIMA RESERVE

7 AERATION SPRAYS

factors have high potential for implementation because of their pragmatic aspect and, in addition, because they have the potential to establish new relationships across many fields.

The final proposal is a series of interventions to catalyse new habits of occupation within the landscape. The tactical nature of the proposal acknowledges the presence of simultaneous, sometimes covert, agendas at play, so that the resulting design is flexible in its degree and means of deployment. Although the planning and built structures were designed to address issues specific to the unique conditions of an embayment along Lake Assad, the project's strategy of acknowledging inherent multilevel operations and using them to produce a matrix of action can be used as a methodology in a global arena. The articulation of a landscape design process that can shift scale between the local and the global was fundamental to the project.

PROPOSAL

1. Fix Position
Planning structure: The situation of an axis for lake-water dispersal is a unifying gesture to promote a community identity – but one that demands a community reassessment of the action of bounding territory. Since depletion of the local ground-water resources necessitates alternative water sourcing, and no single player in the embayment has the money and power to make a large project viable, a coalition must be formed and neutral territory designated. This presents a return to the presettlement political condition in which exploitation of resources was often communally negotiated.
Duration: Permanent and constant.

2. Instigate Cycles of Use and Abandonment
Planning structure: Resources are mobilised and a system of collection, transfer and dispersal projected. Relatively low levels of labour investment allow shifting

Opposite
Map rendering the deployment of the proposed planning and built structures. The network shown is a potential initial iteration of ongoing processes. Not all components would occur simultaneously and the completion of the events does not comprise an end game.

Above left
Vicinity of settlement: existing condition – wet season.

Above right
Vicinity of settlement: transformation. Deep sheet-pile-lined water-retention channels excavated out of seasonal stream channels adjacent to settlements would allow large areas of intensive agriculture to be located near homes to take advantage of waste as compost. *Hima* reserve area is visible up the distant slope.

The proposal is presented as a series of events – an alternative form of zoning or building code. Each planning structure is an independent urban gesture designed to begin implementation of the agenda expressed as its title. Simultaneously, the term structure is used to designate the interrelation of parts forming a complex entity. The events are loosely ordered. Several components cannot be realised at the scale proposed unless certain moves are made to promote community cohesion. But the scale of the gestures is intentionally flexible. Built structures provide physical fields of interaction for politics, infrastructure, environment and culture. The overlap, conflict, and juxtaposition of the proposed physical structures present new challenges to the polity and open up new possibilities for habitation within the landscape. A temporal component is described for each event as an indicator of the return of a spatiotemporal continuum to the region.

demands to be recognised. The trafficking in these resources foments intra-embayment interactions.
Built structure: Traditional water-management meets modern technology as water-storage channels are excavated out of wadi beds. Algae are dredged from the lake and dispersed in fields to dry. The displaced materials are then used as construction resources and fertiliser. The algae are an available organic material that when combined with the decomposing rock will provide a planting mix for use in the gardens and fields. The wadi excavations forge new watercourses and the web of seasonal stream channels is extended. Additional opportunities for trench water-storage accrue within the web of new watercourses.
Duration: Seasonal, transient activity.

3. Shift Courses
Planning structure: Schedule of timed release and rules of flow.
Built structure: An elevated tubular-steel aqueduct is an economical, efficient landmark visible from across the embayment. Once pumped up to the aqueduct from

the lake, the gravity-powered, flexible framework for intensive drip irrigation allows seasonal and crop-specific water use. The functional length of the pipe is determined by the capacity of the available pump and can be increased as economy and technology permit.
Duration: Ongoing, shifting.

4. Radiate a New Spectrum

Planning structure: A pattern of dispersal and access to agricultural land is based on multiple levels of investment and the Islamic system of usufruct. The slope towards the lake, and the distance gravity will propel the falling water through the conduit, determine the limits of the field of gardens.
Built structure: A field of gardens allocated to villages and rented to families. Multiscale plots establish economic diversity along a transect.
Duration: As a whole constant and long term; individual plots go boom and bust.

5. Migrant Construction

Planning structure: Low care, temporary, agricultural infrastructure is encouraged to allow expansion, diminishment or relocation based on shifting hydrology, and supply and demand.
Built structure: Sheet-pile-lined wadi trenches, mobile trench pumps and garden enclosures

make surface water more mobile across the site with varying degrees of permanence.
Duration: Sporadic, transient.

6. Reserve

Planning structure: Hima, or specially protected areas, are set aside for embayment-wide use. This re-establishes a value system of honourable use through internal controls as prescribed by the Koran.
Built structure: Passive – the eroded slopes of the Jebel are preserved from grazing and allowed to revegetate. The accrued breakdown of seasonal vegetation with the decomposing substrate forms new soil. The new surface will ultimately obstruct the current paths of water flow and transform the flood-plain hydrologic arena. Active – set aside an open area for commerce unattached to any single village and visible from the highway. The extraterritorial commercial venue promotes an influx of the exotic.
Duration: As long as needed.

7. Measure Movement

Planning structure: A locally empowered coalition could seek an extraterritorial impact. The Syrian Arab Republic could initiate a move to establish a Euphrates flow regime.
Built structure: Aeration sprays deployed in the lake diminish or halt eutrophication. Increased oxygen levels create an environment that favours animal over plant life. The rise in aquatic life resounds in the villages as another economic resource becomes available.
Duration: Not precipitate, endless in impact. ∆

THE SKY
ABOVE AND

THE GROUND
BELOW
EMSCHER

'The sky above the Ruhr district must become blue again.'
— Willy Brandt, 1961[1]

One of the first efforts in the short history of the current brownfield movement to reclaim the disused industrial environment at a regional scale, Emscher Park in the northern Ruhr district of Germany leaves most of its 10,000 hectares of industrial wasteland, spoil tips, dumps and contaminated ground contaminated. As part of its Leftover Land project, large tracts of industrial wasteland are left to the devices of nature; they are simply recategorised as woods so that the Forest Administration will oversee their care and appropriate use.[2]

Certainly, the Emscher Park International Building Exhibition (IBA Emscher) includes heroic acts of cleanup: a 30-year project by the Emscher River authority to reclaim over 350 kilometres of rivers and streams that had been straightened, levelled, lined with concrete and turned into an open sewer system at the turn of the 20th century; a new state-of-the-art biological sewage treatment plant at the confluence of the Emscher and the Rhine; and the construction of Mottbruch Halde Gladbeck, a heap of 22.4 million tons of excavated waste deposited on an area of about 54 hectares that artists are continually shaping as 'a heap of change'. But, as Karl Ganser, the official voice of IBA Emscher, has said: 'It would have been meaningless to attempt to reclaim all the contaminated land and spend hundreds of thousands of marks and 20 years in the process, to only end up with decontaminated soil but no projects.'[3]

In their contextualised understanding of brownfield, the authors of IBA Emscher viewed contamination as only one of many preconditions in a region shaped by the interaction of geological resources and economy rather than political boundaries. They considered the current 'thinning-out'[4] of the traditional European city into networks of monofunctional environments such as shopping malls, office parks and bedroom communities as a brownfield situation in the making that would be even more resistant to adaptive reuse than Emscher's industrial archaeology. They saw the loose sprawl of the postindustrial Ruhr laid upon a fractured and fissured ground of disused industry and allied worker settlements as an opportunity for a new order, hampered by neither an antiquated armature of cities incapable of logical expansion nor a dense suburban situation difficult to overhaul. Like the first industrialists, they too mined the site but for its latent urbanity as well as for its historical culture.

The image of the industrial ruin in a self-consciously neglected landscape that has come to signify Emscher is but one aspect of a larger reclamation of the region's historical culture. In its broadest sense, Emscher belongs to Germany's late 20th-century efforts in so many arenas to come to terms with its own past. In fact, some of the regional devastation derives from the bombs of the Second World War. Most of the geography of the contamination is, however, the trace of the war between labour and capital.

The Emscher region is vast because industrialists saw the landscape as an open field, unchallenged and without impediment to free-ranging colonisation – a Lebensraum. Structures were erected willy-nilly in the countryside, used until a resource was depleted, the machinery obsolete or the location inconvenient, and then moved. Industry blazed trails of contamination as it moved from south to north, mining, building and discarding. Roads and rails supporting the relocation of industry likewise spread into a dense and overdeveloped network. This shifting ground of employment subjected the region's initially mixed society of agriculture, steel and commerce to an increasingly focused idea of labour, of 'inhabitants who put their lives at the service of progress' and moved along with it from worker settlement to worker settlement.[5] All of this, as Peter Zlonicky writes in the following article, occurs rather late in the history of industrialisation, in the first third of the 20th century, in a brief episode of 30 years.

Simultaneous with the emergence of this spatial structure of industry between 1910 and 1920, a regional authority, the Siedlungsverband Ruhrkohlenbezirk, under the leadership of Robert Schmidt, proposed an alternative structure of landscape to better integrate the cultures of labour and capital, 'a national park for the industrial district of the Rhineland and Westphalia, which is not remote but a belt of meadows and wood easily accessible from all communities, running through the region in as continuous a form as possible'.[6]

While self-consciously placing their work in the great tradition of the German building exhibitions, the authors of IBA Emscher also see themselves as the inheritors of Schmidt's project in a new set of circumstances. Ironically because of their disused state, the six north–south trails of contamination running across the east–west spine of the polluted

water system become the new green armature for the connection of 17 existing towns spread over an area of 800 square kilometres. As in the original plan, the landscape is to function as the infrastructure of planning and the catalyst for the renewed integration of environment, work and dwelling outlined in Zlonicky's three-part programme. The socioeconomic trends of the preceding 30 years – contraction of industry, rise of unemployment and decline in population within an increasingly mobile society – make this task of reintegration more dramatically a task of economic reconstruction, if not the creation of an entire new culture of labour.

In the climate of the 1980s economic boom – Emscher's so-called 'heroic' phase – the authors of IBA took on the creation of a new culture of labour not by the direct force of a traditional master plan, which they believed would fail the economic task, but by the indirect strategy of the 'integrated project', single developments of environment, work or dwelling that nevertheless contribute to all three programmes.

IBA had the authority to define both the projects and their performance criteria, to which the private developer or private/ public partnership was then accountable. It structured the initial series of projects according to the three programmatic themes: 'The Landscape Park' initiated eight model park projects along the seven green corridors; 'Ecological Regeneration' focused on the reclamation of 350 kilometres of waste water for recreational and utilitarian use; 'Working in the Park' designated 22 former industrial sites for development as service, commercial or new ecotechnology and industrial hubs; 'New Use for Industrial Buildings' applied the principles of 'working in the park' to seven existing industrial structures slated for public cultural uses like museums; 'Housing and Integrated

Notes
1 Quoted by Karl Ganser in an interview with Robert Schäfer in 'IBA Emscher Park: A motor for structural change', Topos, vol 26, March 1999, p 9.
2 Jorg Dettmar, 'Wilderness or park?', Topos, op cit, pp 31–42.
3 Karl Ganser , op cit, p 14.
4 Thomas Sieverts, 'Urban network and townscape: Is the Emscher region a model for the city of the 21st century?' in Change Without Growth: Culture of Building of Cities in the 21st Century, Vieweg (Wisbaden), 1997, p 48.
5 Ingrid Stoppa-Sehlbach, 'The architecture of the everyday: Aesthetics of industrial culture in the Ruhr-Emscher region', in Change Without Growth, op cit, p 54.
6 Michael Schwarze Rodrian, 'Intercommunal co-operation in the Emscher Landscape Park, Topos, op cit, p 54.
7 These themes are those described in the IBA Emscher publication from the project's 'halfway point'. Marion Zerressen et al, The Emscher Park International Building Exhibition, IBA Emscher Park (Gelsenkirchen), 1996.
8 Karl Ganser, 'Architecture as process: the International Building Exhibition Emscher Park', in Change Without Growth, op cit, p 80.
9 Ibid, p 78.
10 Ibid, p 80.

Urban District Development' began as 26 housing projects equally divided between the restoration of historical worker settlements and the creation of new housing that would reinvent settlement principles.[7]

These thematic developments shared certain criteria and strategies of implementation, enumerated by Zlonicky as IBA's greatest legacy. The final strategy on Zlonicky's list and the one that took on increasing importance as the economic picture understood as 'a comprehensive design and building task'.[8]

For Ganser, even a single building of such quality 'stands as an unrenounceable element in the environmental and economic regeneration strategy'.[9] He describes how the strategies of IBA led to the almost spontaneous emergence of quality at Lanferbach when 'the hydraulic engineers let themselves be infected by the spirit of *baukultur* at the construction site and engaged not only civil engineers but a water designer as well, whose task it was to lend

The greatest threat to the new *Baukultur* of the Emscher region is the arrival of investors bent on conventional large-scale development who, like the industrialist colonisers of the last century, are uncomprehending of the integrated landscape they find before them.

of Germany faltered, is the strategy of 'quality'. Quality refers to aesthetic quality, quality of building design and construction, but it also refers to quality of life, which the IBA authors describe as bound up with these physicalities. In the first 'heroic' phase they tried to implement the link between quality of building and quality of life directly, by using the 'integrated project' to provide employment both during and after construction and to build local community through user participation in all phases of programming and design. This integration of the worker and the work constituted a new *Baukultur*, a term associated with a pre-industrial craft but now

an artistic touch to the ecological necessity of regenerating this body of water to a near natural state. Eventually the mining company became interested in a "tailing heap work of art", which was developed as a limited competition for visual artists.'[10]

For Zlonicky, the greatest threat to the new *Baukultur* of the Emscher region is not the decline in population from 6 million in 1962 to 4.5 million and dropping in 1999, nor the concomitant strategy of 'change without growth', but rather the arrival of investors bent on conventional large-scale development in the troubled wake of Emscher's first revitalisation who, like the industrialist colonisers of the last century, are uncomprehending of the integrated landscape they find before them.

Deborah Gans

Strategies for Extreme Conditions:
The Emscher Park International Building Exhibition

The 10-year mandate of IBA Emscher was nothing less than to initiate an even grander 20- to 30-year economic and physical reconstruction of a largely contaminated region of the industrial Ruhr region encompassing 17 towns along 70 kilometres of the Emscher River. As an author of the project, **Peter Zlonicky** describes how by effecting model projects rather than rendering a single master plan, IBA Emscher managed to load the landscape with certain large-scale armatures, such as greenways; certain ways of life, such as 'working in the park'; and certain values and qualities, such as *Baukultur*, that can shape its future perhaps more effectively than either conventional economic development or policy approaches to brownfields.

Opening spread
Aerial view of the Emscher–Rurh
valley along its reclaimed river
and greenway.

Top
**Aerial view towards Duisburg-
Nord Landscape Park, 1994**
Landscape architects: Latz and
Partner Architects. Engineers:
Peter Poelzig, AG Höhmann
& Pahl-Weber-Pahl, Bähr
and Spitzenboom, BauCoop
Artur Mandler, Düster & von
Büttner, Günter Lipkowsky.
Lighting design: Jonathan Park
The park occupies 200 hectares
of brownfield in one of the
designated green corridors
running between the districts of
Meiderich and Hamborn. While
the river and particular sites have
been reconstructed, much of the
landscape is left to spontaneous
growth. There are marked routes of
industrial archaeology and culture
as well as cycle and walking paths
that connect the corridor to the
larger landscape structure
covering a total of 270 kilometres.
The preserved Meiderich smelting
plants are now landmarks in the
western Emscher valley. The park's
topographic and cultural focal point
is the former Thyssen steelworks.

Bottom
Masterplan Emscher
Landschaftspark 2010 (2003)

The Emscher region is one of the most important industrial heartlands of Europe. In contrast to the southern Ruhr Region, industrialisation here got off to a late start, but was pursued recklessly and on a grand scale. The crisis of heavy industries in Europe had outstanding dimensions in the Emscher region. Ravaged landscape, urban decay and widespread brownfields were evidence of the need for structural change.

Germany has a remarkable tradition in innovative building exhibitions, from the Darmstadt artist's colony of 1901, to Siedlungen of the 1920s to the Berlin Hansa quarter of 1957. Recognising their strength and adopting them as a model, IBA Berlin (1984–7) placed the emphasis on social strategies to rebuild Kreuzberg, a part of the city in crisis. Why should it not be possible to extend local to regional renewal? Why not 'tidy up'[1] the Ruhr district's backyard with an international exchange of best-practice experiences, extending the classical sense of exhibitions?

So IBA Emscher, the Emscher Park International Building Exhibition, was established as a 10-year programme to identify new perspectives for the future of an economically and socially weakened region. Within this short range of time the IBA activities realised some remarkable changes. This essay asks: 'What are its sustainable achievements, and which of its perspectives can be recognised today?'

1989: The Heroic Start
At the end of the 1980s, former strategies of regional renewal came to an end. There was no future for the endless subsidies to heavy industry; there was no need for public infrastructures serving industrial development; and there was no hope of replacing old large-scale industries with large-scale new industries. So a small group of politicians and planners came to the conclusion that a widespread ecological renewal must precede any lasting economic revival. Our hopes grew in light of political changes such as *perestroika* and international economic developments like the Blue Banana of Britain and the Mediterranean Sunbelt,[2] both of which touched the Ruhr. The migration from eastern European countries to Germany raised the number of inhabitants even in the Emscher region. And the emerging model of public-private partnership became an important issue in a process of structural change. Established under these social and economic conditions, the IBA agency, an institution owned by the *Land* of North Rhine Westphalia with private-sector status, and thus a quasi-nongovernmental organisation (quango) of only some 25 employees, set its task in Emscher according to certain themes summarised in the following programmes:

1. Landscape and watercourses are to be seen as a new infrastructure apart from the classical industry-oriented infrastructure. Industrial monuments convey a message of identity; they are landmarks in a landscape devoid of orientation.
2. Residential uses are to be provided, including innovations with mixed uses on brownfield sites and the maintenance of the existing stock, especially the old workers' cottages with garden-city features.

3. New forms and new qualities of work are to be offered at the old sites but with higher standards of education and environment. There must be space for new social and cultural activities, especially in transforming industrial monuments to a new identity.

After formulating basic-position papers concerning ecology, economic, architectural, cultural and social standards of regional renewal along the lines of these three programme points, the IBA published a call for ideas, which was answered by more than 400 citizens and institutions in the region. A tight cooperation of private investors and public administration – the IBA serving as moderator and quality surveyor – began to realise some 40 projects, each dealing with small-scale contributions to the larger programmes.

This 'heroic' start of the IBA was affected by the fall of the Berlin Wall. National strategies for rebuilding eastern Germany became more important than structural changes in western Germany, and highly subsidised private investment in the former GDR became much more profitable than any investment in the Emscher region. Due to these events public engagement had to replace private investment

1994: Change Without Growth!
The five-year 'halfway' presentation of the IBA activities was successful. Congresses with international participation strengthened the personal network of cooperation and exchange. Exhibitions in the IBA agency, situated in a former colliery, were accompanied by local events in the 17 cities presenting their IBA projects.

However, in 1994 the short period of economic growth came to an end. Demographic

In 1994 the short period of economic growth came to an end. Demographic growth changed to decline. No further investment in big housing projects was needed; housing problems turned into vacancy problems. Companies required subsidies to rationalise production and then continued operation with half of their former staff, leaving an urban and social desert on their former sites.

growth changed to decline. No further investment in big housing projects was needed; housing problems turned into vacancy problems. Companies required subsidies to rationalise production and then continued operation with half of their former staff, leaving an urban and social desert on their former sites. IBA did not continue producing new buildings; rather it looked seriously at small-scale changes in the existing landscape and in the existing built stock as its basis for ecological, social and cultural improvement and as a more adequate contribution to sustainable development. Artists were invited to define new identities and to set landmarks. A new motto was formulated – Change Without Growth. This became the central message and remains so today.

Below left
Thyssen steelworks, now the Duisburg-Nord Landscape Park, 1994
The smelting and coke works of the plant have been reconstituted as theatrical settings of sound and light, a mning history centre and a variety of cultural uses. The 200 hectares of brownfield in which they are set is landscape based on the spontaneous vegetation that had grown up with the abandonment of the plants in the mid-1980s.

Below right
Meiderich smelting plant, 1994
The topographic centre of the Duisburg-Nord Landscape Park is this former plant, now abandoned but preserved.

The final activity in the Emscher Region summed up 10 years' experience in transforming urban landscape and life. As the Emscher Park authority ended in 1999, local politicians in the Ruhr region seemed to prefer new types of big projects, reinventing former strategies of big-scale investment as a solution for big-scale problems.

1999: Conflicting Strategies

The final activity in the Emscher region summed up 10 years' experience in transforming urban landscape and life. As the Emscher Park authority ended in 1999, local politicians in the Ruhr region seemed to prefer new types of big projects, reinventing former strategies of big-scale investment as a solution for big-scale problems. The CentrO in Oberhausen, a 75,000-square-metre shopping mall supplemented by cinemas, sports and other entertainment attractions had an observed effect on the decay of the traditional city centre. Yet the economic success of the CentrO stimulated similar projects in Duisburg, Essen and especially in Dortmund. The current struggles between new and traditional centres, 'mega malls' and small-scale structures, 'American' and 'European' city models will be overshadowed, it seems, by the emerging struggle between mega mall and mega mall.

Are the IBA strategy of stimulating endogenous potentials and the strategy of big investments seen as competing and mutually exclusive or as corresponding strategies? Do big investments eliminate local potentials, or do they offer a reduction of commercial pressure that offers an opportunity for mixed uses, living and working, social and cultural functions in the old city?

2004: Achievements to Remain

Due to globalisation and privatisation, a new period of urban poverty prevents further large-scale projects from being realised. A corresponding new appreciation for IBA's philosophies and successes over its 10-year mandate has emerged, inspiring the North Rhine Westphalia government to transfer IBA strategies to other areas in the state. Budgets are offered on the condition that regions establish boards of regional actors to formulate appropriate strategies and oversee the realisation of projects that may contribute to modernisation. They have established a Regionale, a composition of Region and Biennale, to occur in two-year sequences up to 2010. An Institute of European City Culture intended to encourage best practices in urban projects has been founded in a former colliery.

The impact of IBA Emscher continues to grow though its official period of action has concluded. Former members of the IBA staff go on to work in such offshoot institutes as the Institute of European City Culture, in the Regionale agencies, in universities and in public administrations disseminating IBA experiences. International exchanges continue with other European regions, and with academic institutions in the US working on brownfield conversion projects. Tourism and cultural events, including the Ruhr Trienniale, theatre, music and dance productions realised by the former Salzburg festival director on reclaimed industrial sites, have become new economic factors in the Emscher region and

Above
Haldenereignis Emscherblick, Bottrop. Stone dump with a View, 1996
Designers: Christ and Bollingen
Engineers: Jürgen LIT Fischer
Lighting designers: Drecker
Office Landscape
The waste stone dump located in green corridor C is a pile from the Prosper 11 pit that was dumped on former farmland. It is now partially covered with vegetation and impressed with a 65-metre steeply terraced plateau that leads to the 60-metre tetrahedral viewing platform.

Right, top and bottom
Siedlung Schüngelberg workers' housing, Gelsenkirchen, 1919–28; extension 1993–7
Original architect: JOHOW
New extension: Rolf Keller
Built for the families of workers in the Zeche Hugo coal mines, this 'garden city' was not completed, left as it was by German families in the 1970s, before being taken over by Turkish families in the 1980s. In cooperation with the residents, the Treuhandstelle für Bergarbeiterwohnungsbau restored the existing buildings and the environment (1992–96), and a new extension was added after an IBA competition won by Swiss architect Rolf Keller. The ecological standards here are high.

Above
Working in Emscher Park, 1993
Under the auspices of the IBA, 22 different sites covering 500 hectares have been designated as locations of offices, laboratories and service industries. They are implemented as joint public–private ventures, according to precise specifications for environmental performance, green spaces and amenities. The image on the left is the Future Centre and Technology Park in Herten (architects Rüdiger Kramm and Axel Strigl). The project on the right is the Technology Centre for Environmental Protection, Oberhausen.

Notes
1 'Tidy up the Ruhr' is a popular slogan of the IBA Emscher project.
2 The Blue Banana refers to the curve of blue light visible via satellite that stretches across the former industrial heartland of Europe from the UK to Italy. It is now used to describe the shape of a new emerging economic spine that follows the old geography. The Mediterranean Sunbelt refers to parallel geography, based on sun and water, that is an emerging regional economic development.

attract thousands of visitors daily.

Despite the general economic downturn within Germany, the Emscher region has emerged as first in research and production of solar energy. The traditional use of regional potentials – producing energy by mining – has switched to the endless potentials of producing energy by innovation.

Perhaps the most precious heritage of IBA, however, is a set of strategies in conflict with traditional planning methods that resulted from its continuous learning processes over its 10-year lifetime:

· **Reforms without reform!**
We didn't wait until politicians were ready to improve administration processes and planning laws.
· **Projects, no formal plans!**
Although the results of formal, hierarchical planning were correct, they did not generate quality. Project planning allows quality control. A new generation of planners will learn from this approach.
· **Sustainability without textbooks!**
Criteria for sustainable development have to be fixed on a project-by-project basis according to the specific site conditions.
· **Energy without coal!**
This is meant as a rhetorical, general

provocation to any form of traditional mentality found in regional economy and politics, but also as a real change to solar energy.
· **Quality by moderation!**
The results of participatory processes have to be fixed by quality contracts with the developers who win responsibility for the project.

Whatever future developments of endogenous and exogenous strategies may be, IBA projects are yardsticks of planners' and citizens' awareness. They engendered:

· A new regard for industrial heritage as a potential for cultural identification, and for brownfields as a potential for sustainable development.
· A new appreciation of landscape and water as 'soft' regional infrastructures, more important to further development than former 'hard' infrastructures.
· A new experience in the potentials of cooperation among local and regional actors, and in their mediation of planning and implementing processes.
· A new estimation of culture and art as essential elements of regional identity.
· A new sense of the beauty of the region, of its specific aesthetic values.
· A new and surprising recognition of the potentials for innovation in a noninnovative milieu.

All in all: more than 100 projects executed, stars illuminating a path to future sustainable development. ᗤ

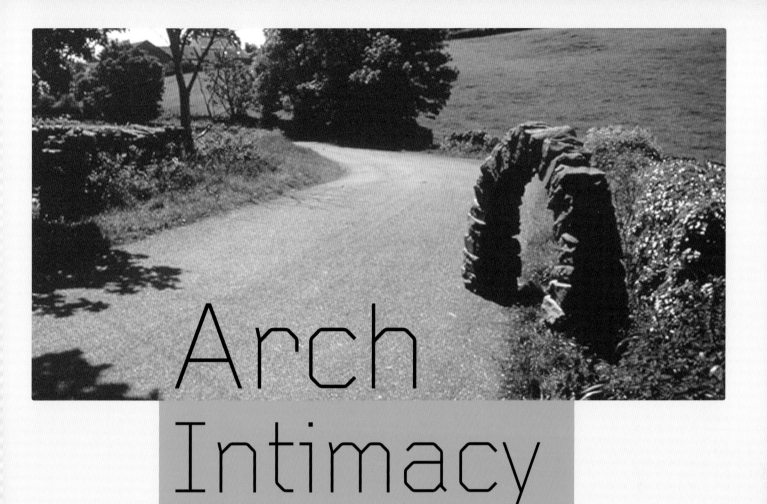

Arch Intimacy

The work of Andy Goldsworthy allows us to see the pastoral and the agrarian as mined landscapes, according to this essay by **Matthew Jelacic**. Goldsworthy's work is a lens through which to assess the impact of the economy and industry of herding on the environment. Like the recuperation of Emscher's industrial artefacts, it is also a vehicle of collective memory.

Above
Andy Goldsworthy's arch at Fellside, Kirkby Lonsdale, Cumbria (17 June 1997), built here between an ancient drove-route wall on the right and sheepfold on the left. Straddling the verdant agrarian landscape and the macadam belt that bisects it, it is one of 22 reconstructions of the Arch.

'There are worse places to work,' says Andy. 'Everywhere is a worse place to work,' I suggest. He eyes the drop into the sheepfold ground and says, 'Well, it'll be a job getting the stones down there.'[1]

Andy Goldsworthy constructed his *Arch* no less than 22 times along an ancient route once used for transporting sheep from open grazing lands in northern Dumfries and Galloway to slaughterhouses, markets and ports in southern Lancashire. Along these historic routes, or 'droves', were built a series of holding pens, or 'folds'. Goldsworthy's *Arch* was usually located in proximity to existing, dilapidated or imagined archeological folds. Construction was completed in a day and photographed and deconstructed the next, ready to be moved to the subsequent site.

The drove routes and folds are symbolically important to Goldsworthy because of their identification with an extinct way of life that relied on the working relationship of man with the earth. Today cars and lorries have replaced the sheep in the droves, and the folds are mostly left to ruin. Building the *Arch* on the sites of the folds allowed Goldsworthy to engage with people who might have knowledge of other local vestiges of the agrarian industrial constructions, but more importantly it allowed him the chance to reintroduce people to the traces of their landscape that are all that remain of the cultural convulsion we call the Agricultural Revolution.

An important, subtle condition of the *Arch* project is that the sites of droves and folds are typically much older than the partitioning walls that came with the Enclosure Acts that began in the 18th century. While economists have exhausted this era mining for the origins of 'the market', sociologists and ecologists have traditionally and more quietly understood that revolution to mark the end of *Landschaft*. Neither merely a spatial organisation nor a systematic governance, *Landschaft* encompassed an idea that families were responsible for their neighbours and the environment equally, and that this shared responsibility constituted community.

Medieval agrarian production was conducted in common fields, called the demesne, surrounding small

61

collections of loosely grouped houses. In this manorial system, the land was communally divided, every family having responsibilities on the lord's land as well as growing their own food. Livestock, including cows as well as sheep, was left to graze on the meagre stubble of the demesne after the autumn harvest. All but the breeding livestock would be driven to market and sold, as most would be unable to withstand winter for lack of fodder.

The value of English wool, most of which came from young sheep and was thus very fine, rose dramatically, such that by the 12th century large-scale farmers, especially the Church, were bounding very large sheep runs. The export value of the wool was to make up a majority of the nation's wealth until the 14th century when home production began to have an influence on social as well as economic trends. By the beginning of the 16th century Sir Thomas More wrote: 'Sheep have become so great devourers and so wild that they eat up and swallow down the very men themselves. They consume, destroy and devour whole fields, houses and cities.'[2] Landowners, able to increase the profitability of their land with the low labour costs and high returns of grazing sheep began to remove families from the demesne and their ancestral homes and build the great droves that characterised the English landscape, especially in the West Country. By the time Elizabeth I toured her country she found that: 'Paupers are everywhere.'[3] Yeomen, without arable fields to tend, had few alternatives but to live on the streets of the small towns.

By the 17th century, small experiments in crop rotation and animal husbandry began to have an effect in agrarian production. These experiments gained popularity as the yield of crops increased dramatically, and they also initiated an equally dramatic movement, the Land Enclosure Acts, which meant selective breeding and crop boundaries could be better controlled and the land commodified for sale or lease. The crop-rotation system yielded dependable winter fodder so that larger numbers of sheep could be kept through the winter.

The residual effects of the Agricultural Revolution on the wool industry are not surprising. The commodity value of wool rose at a greater rate than any other agricultural product. The number of sheep increased by a third, but their value increased by 590 per cent as the value of mutton was added, thanks to efficient transport to markets and breeding that selected advantageous ratios of bone to meat.[4] As populations expanded with the increase in grain-crop production, demand for wool and fresh mutton rose accordingly. The increased profitability of the sheep resulted in more sweeping alterations to the landscape as a true agricultural industry was born.

But these advances came with other costs. The quality of the wool coarsened as sheep grew winter coats. The varieties of sheep decreased as selective breeding homogenised the livestock. By 1850, upwards of 75 per cent of the arable land was rented on short-term leases,[5] and this commodification of the land suddenly made the ancient drove routes untenable as landowners began to charge tolls and grazing charges for the grassy edges that the common wide paths had afforded. 'By 1850 most of the green arteries were disused. The traffic moved first to sailing boats, then to steamers. In their holds a horrific number of animals smothered and died.'[6]

And this created the background for the Arch project.

In Stone, Goldsworthy describes the influence of agrarian dry-stone walls on his thinking and working. He explicitly focuses on the importance of the walls' construction and on the relationship of the walls to livestock. In Arch there is a formal translation of the wall and a conceptual translation of the sheep, both explicitly made. Formally, the wall of a curved fold is rotated about its horizontal axis. Standing the wall upright as an arch focuses attention on the techné of the stonemason. Goldsworthy requires that his walls be 'simple (but beautiful)'.[7] The scale and juxtaposition of the red sandstone arch and the fragmented remnants of the old grey stones of the folds and droves not only creates a strong visual contrast but also stands in for transplanted sheep with a northern migrant material. Continuously his narrative describes the Arch as an animal, alive and moving.

Below
The Arch, here reconstructed in Carlisle, Cumbria, acts as an emissary for the lost agrarian landscape in a resonant location.

Top left
The agrarian landscape has been subsumed by new technologies. Goldsworthy's project mediates these ideas of landscape through the systematic reconstruction of the *Arch*.

Top right
The scale and juxtaposition of the red sandstone arch and fragmented remnants of the old grey stones of the folds and droves not only creates a strong visual contrast but also stands in for transplanted sheep with a northern migrant material.

Bottom
Goldsworthy and team working to get voussoirs to a new site.

Notes
1 Andy Goldsworthy and David Craig, *Arch*, Abrams (New York), 1999, p 78.
2 L Dudley Stamp, *Man and the Land*, Collins (London), 1964, p 64.
3 Robert L Heilbroner, *The Worldly Philosophers*, Simon & Schuster (New York), 1961, p 18.
4 Mark Overton, *Agricultural Revolution in England*, Cambridge University Press (London), 1996, p 165.
5 Ibid, p 185.
6 Goldsworthy, op cit, p 32.
7 Andy Goldsworthy, *Stone*, Abrams (New York), 1994, p 106.
8 Goldsworthy, *Arch*, p 74.

However, assessing the project in terms other than the motivations of the imagery or the historic context of its construction grounds the object in a more tangible and contemporary critique of social and environmental conditions. The temporality of the constructions required two things of Goldsworthy. The most obvious requirement was documentation. The project exists now only through the evidence of the wonderful photographs, journal and text of his co-author. This mode of representation is typical of the majority of Goldsworthy's work, much of which is projected, recorded and expected to evaporate.

The second requirement of the artist was a great deal of physical labour, and it is this 'work' that differentiates *Arch* from other of Goldsworthy's projects and makes more potent the critique the project launches. The stones for *Arch* were commissioned, carved at a stoneyard to create a kit of parts. Unlike his other walls, he does not rely on the labour of skilled masons to complete the construction of *Arch*: the project's assembly, disassembly and transportation are completed by a small team – Goldsworthy playing a central role in the labour force. In this way the production of the *Arch* is mechanised – akin to the industrial-era production of agriculture and factory work alike.

Consistently he is concerned that the *Arch* project will be ill-received in the communities within which he is working, and without exception 'the arch is a great ambassador for the project'.[8] The reason for this is ultimately not acknowledged in the documentation, and reflects a certain lack of assuredness about the larger meaning of the project for Goldsworthy. However, between the lines and in the candid photos of the construction process a clearer portrait of the importance and cultural meaning of the work arises.

Repetitive reconstruction allows an intimacy with the '29 stones' of the *Arch*, and this knowledge of the piece intensifies the relationship with the sites by allowing a spontaneity and virtuosity of construction that pays homage to the memory of the original work of the sites. As with the peasants and yeomen before him, intense physical and personal labour yields a communal recognition and cooperation, and thus *Arch* allows Goldsworthy to bridge over a thousand years of increasing disenfranchisement with the land.

The great achievement of *Arch* was to recognise that the decrepitude of the failing proto-brownfield sites of the English Agricultural Revolution could be mediated through intimate, repetitive and small-scale work. The continuously reconstructed juxtaposition of the arch against the technological landscape of modernised agriculture and the transportation routes that subsumed the droves creates a synthetic view of psychic remediation. The project becomes a portal for local communities to re-envision their historical landscape in terms of contemporary, personal and environmental interactions. △

MICHAEL SORKIN STUDIO: SÜDRAUM LEIPZIG 1994

The ecorhetoric of 'greening the brownfield' can be disingenuous in light of the lucrative outcome of urban brownfield redevelopment, and reductive in view of the complex culture of the sites. These sites come loaded with aura: the sublime disaster, the pastoralised ruin, the tabula rasa, the Faustian sinkhole of ambition. **Michael Sorkin**'s Leipzig sublimates our sins against the landscape into a beautiful dreamy city, like a Venice, and so redeems them. And yet, because the city floats upon our past follies so literally, potential ruin might still lurk in its depths. Südraum Leipzig brings a utopic discourse to our understanding of brownfields, and correspondingly reveals the extent to which this discourse is already present in such events as the cleansed waters of Emscher and the cleansing waters of the Indore River.

Opposite
Aerial view of the Südraum Leipzig with the city of Leipzig at the top. The moonscape of abandoned open-pit mines dominates the landscape. Also visible is the already extensive natural filling of the craters by water.

The landscape south of Leipzig – once a picturesque landscape of villages, waterways, wetlands, forest and fields – is now dominated by a series of huge, abandoned, open-pit soft coal (lignite) mines. Although an economic and environmental disaster, this astonishing moonscape is tremendously powerful as visual and cultural artefact, and offers a crumbling museum of the industrial monoculture of mine pits, slag heaps, briquetting works, energy generation, chemical plants, railways and the rusting carcasses of dinosaurian machinery. Although mining began as early as the 17th century, current conditions are largely the product of the 20th. Since the 1920s, 12 cubic kilometres of earth have been moved, entailing the destruction of 60 settlements, the forcible relocation of 24,000 people – and causing enormous pollution.

Our proposal is to allow the mines to fill with water (a process well under way) and to use the old machines to dig channels connecting them into a chain of lakes. This water connection – extending into the centre of Leipzig – would form a new circulation armature for the towns and villages of the Südraum and a site for new villages to replace those lost to the mines. By recontouring the perimeters of the mines to accommodate 'island villages' just offshore, the entire edge of the lakes would be saved for public use and access. The new water-related development, it is hoped, would inspire a distinctive style of life, an interconnected island culture of boats and bridges, with a high degree of sustainability, a rich mix of uses, recreational activities close by and direct access to green space. By freezing construction on nonreclaimed sites, the existing landscape would be protected, threatening urban sprawl contained and a unique pattern of settlement created on the new islands reclaimed from the mines. △D

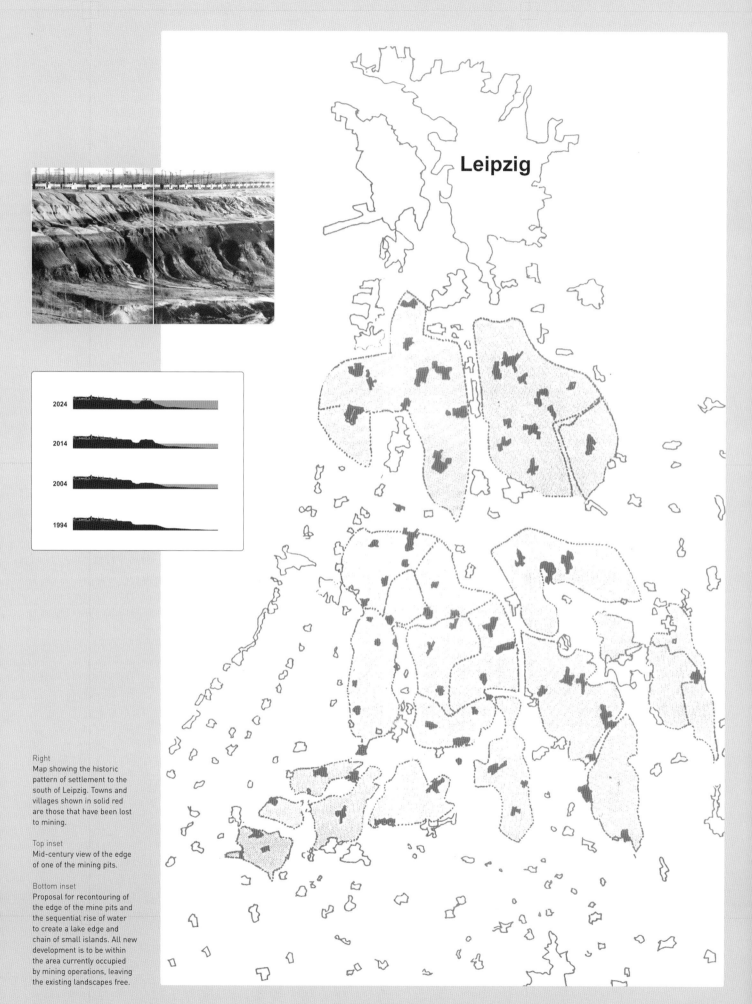

Leipzig

2024

2014

2004

1994

Right
Map showing the historic
pattern of settlement to the
south of Leipzig. Towns and
villages shown in solid red
are those that have been lost
to mining.

Top inset
Mid-century view of the edge
of one of the mining pits.

Bottom inset
Proposal for recontouring of
the edge of the mine pits and
the sequential rise of water
to create a lake edge and
chain of small islands. All new
development is to be within
the area currently occupied
by mining operations, leaving
the existing landscapes free.

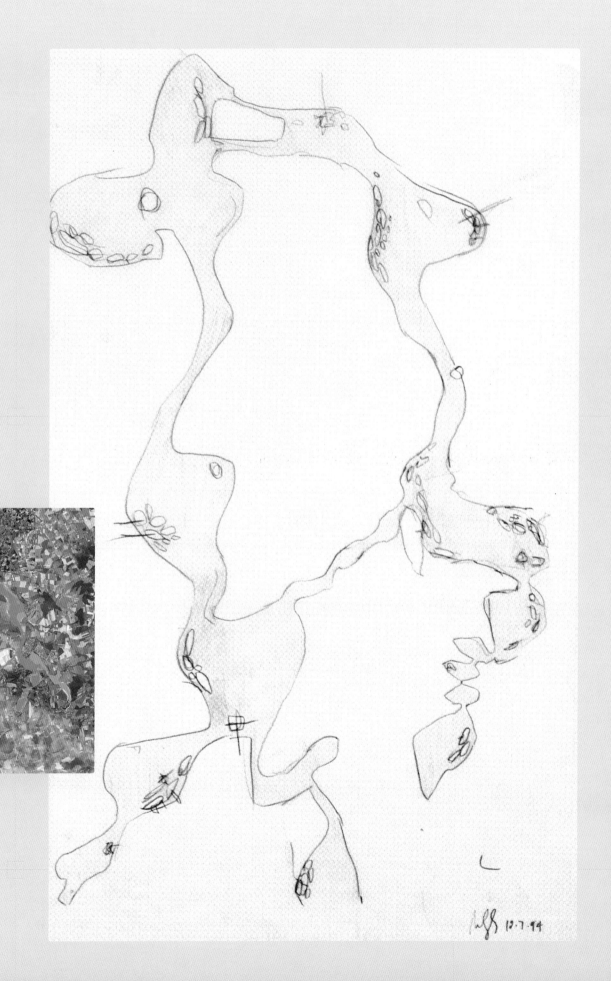

Right
A first sketch of the chain of lakes to be created by connecting the sequence of flooded mines. New development is distributed on a series of islands and peninsulas at the edges of the new lakes.

Inset
The chain of lakes in relationship to the city of Leipzig. Joining the lakes with canals, and the system as a whole to existing waterways, will create an extensive system of waterborne transit and recreation. This will join the new communities to be built and the core of Leipzig into a single network.

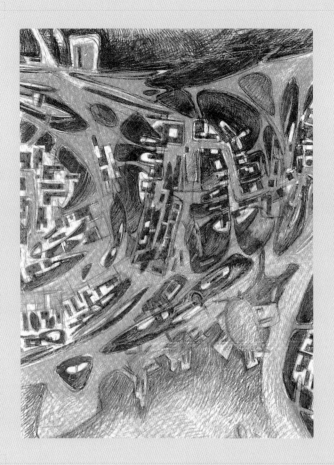

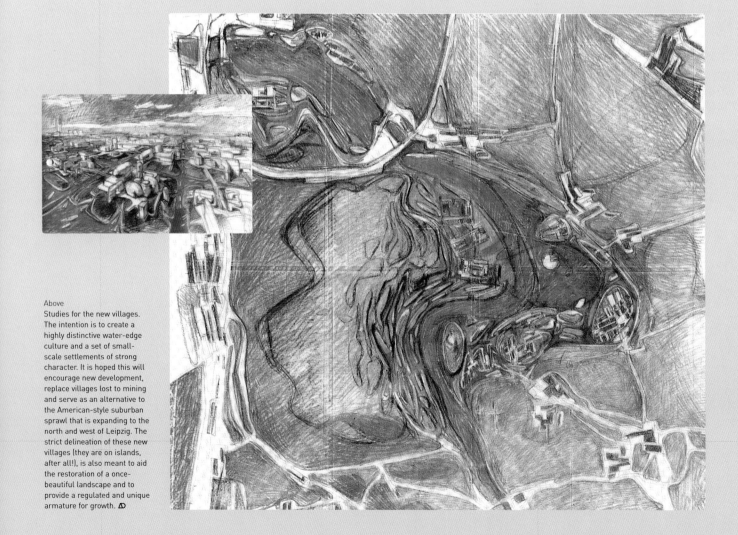

Above
Studies for the new villages. The intention is to create a highly distinctive water-edge culture and a set of small-scale settlements of strong character. It is hoped this will encourage new development, replace villages lost to mining and serve as an alternative to the American-style suburban sprawl that is expanding to the north and west of Leipzig. The strict delineation of these new villages (they are on islands, after all!), is also meant to aid the restoration of a once-beautiful landscape and to provide a regulated and unique armature for growth. ⊅

A hill where it was flat, a park where it was arid, a field for community where there was none. These accomplishments are fitting of Israel's early history, where the act of settlement entailed similar intensive acts of land formation and cultivation in search of a better world. The difference herein is the raw condition of the site, a pile of our own waste, the new post-industrial brownfield as Laura Starr describes it.

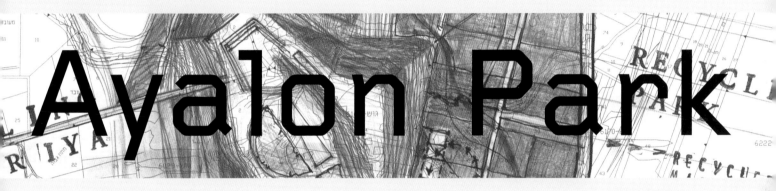

Ayalon Park

Her blow by blow narrative of the Ayalon Park's yet ongoing design and implementation gives us a model for 'how to' rally socio-political, cultural, economic resources around the cause of the urban environment and to create ecological and community consciousness in the process. Still, the facts of this Herculean international effort mobilized to ponder the fundamental quandary of the cultural, social and aesthetic of a garbage dump in the body of expanding Tel Aviv, might warn us against its easy global replication. Perhaps Ayalon should include among its other simultaneously lovely and didactic landscapes a garden of contemplation on the nature of waste.

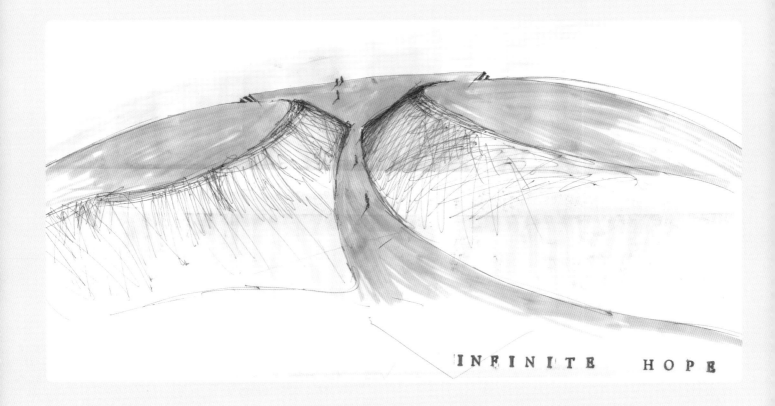

INFINITE   HOPE

In the middle of Israel's largest and densest urban district lies a vast tract of undeveloped land and within it, Hiriya, a mountain of garbage rising 250 feet and covering over 125 acres. From this toxic mesa and the agricultural lands surrounding it, designers envision creating an urban park that will rival New York's Central Park and the Bois de Boulogne, Hyde Park and other internationally known parks in scale and in visibility. While these parks were created in response to dense, unhealthy conditions that the industrial era imposed on people, Ayalon Park will be born out of the urgent post-industrial necessity to remedy the impact of our modern, disposable lifestyle on the land. Its expression will evolve from a forged landscape architectural and engineering language that articulates the challenges of the site -its climate and location, its extreme ecological demands and its body politic.

The site, at the gateway to Tel Aviv is striking in its blankness and contrasts. The park is aptly named for the Ayalon River, whose winter floodwaters have created and protected a flat plain of rich farmland sandwiched between the Tel Aviv's urbanized sandy hills. Cited in the bible, "...Sun, stand thou still upon Giveon; and thou, Moon, in the valley of Ayalon" (Joshua, Chapter 10, 12), the river embodies biblical connotations of wandering (the riverbed) and settling (the cultivated lands) as it carries water from the Judean Hills to the Mediterranean.

Hiriya rises out of this flatness as an eerie piece of land art, a monumental symbol of our throwaway culture at the nexus of Israel's major highways and on axis with the flight path to Ben Gurion Airport. For nearly 50 years Tel Aviv's garbage was dumped here, until in 1998, the dump had to be closed. Unstable slopes threatened to slide into the Ayalon River; poisons were leaching into ground water; and scavenging birds posed a danger to air traffic. The dump now contains 30 million cubic meters of garbage.

My involvement with the project began in September 2000, when I received a letter from Israel that very simply described a complicated situation:

"The Southern Tel Aviv area contains an open space on circa 2000 acres. On the eastern side of it there is a large landfill (garbage dump). Recently a number of artists were asked to come up with proposals to change the dump into an interesting new site open to the public... Simultaneously the district planning office of the Tel Aviv area started promoting the idea of turning the whole area around and including the landfill into the main metropolitan park upgrading the southern part of the metropolitan area."

The letter was from Dr. Martin Weyl who as director of the Israel Museum built an institution that exhibits a continuum or artifacts from the Dead Sea Scrolls to the steel planes of Richard Serra and now, as director of the Baracha Foundation, began to apply his curatorial vision and financial acumen to the creation of a park forged by an international group of "outstanding people from the world of parks". Along side his curatorial efforts, a planning team, led by District Planner Naomi

The site, at the gateway to Tel Aviv is striking in its blankness and contrasts. The park is aptly named for the Ayalon River, whose winter floodwaters have created and protected a flat plain of rich farmland sandwiched between the Tel Aviv's urbanized sandy hills.

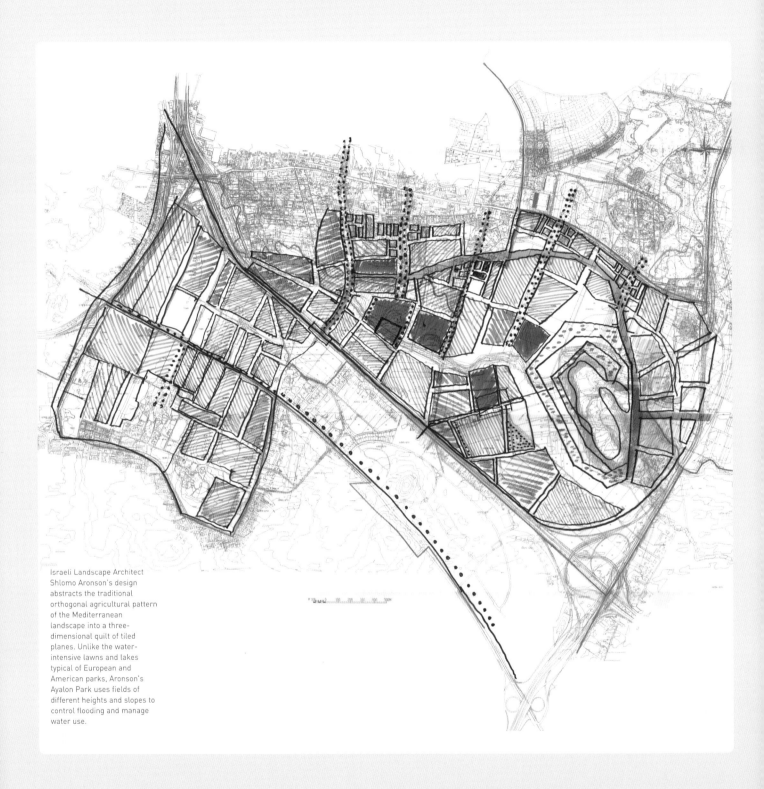

Israeli Landscape Architect
Shlomo Aronson's design
abstracts the traditional
orthogonal agricultural pattern
of the Mediterranean
landscape into a three-
dimensional quilt of tiled
planes. Unlike the water-
intensive lawns and lakes
typical of European and
American parks, Aronson's
Ayalon Park uses fields of
different heights and slopes to
control flooding and manage
water use.

1:2000

N

WASTE WATER TREATMENT WETLAND PARK

AYALON

TREATED SEWAGE FROM THE PLANT

GROUND WATER RECHARGE

HIRIYA

WINTER PONDS

DEEP MARSH

SHALLOW MARSH + TREATMENT

SHALLOW MARSH

DEEP MARSH OPEN WATER

LEACHATE FROM THE MOUNTAIN

CONTROL WEIR

FARM

SAPARIA

WATER

Like many of designs that came out of the charrette, this plan finds inspiration in the seasonal flow of water through the site. The plan features a system of wetlands, some of which will filter Hiriya's leachate; a wadi with retention areas to replenish groundwater and provide water for wildlife in the winter; and a reservoir surrounded by steps designed to reduce evaporation and create beautiful settings for recreation. Drawing: Ken Smith, Robert France, Amir Balaban, and Stephen Handel.

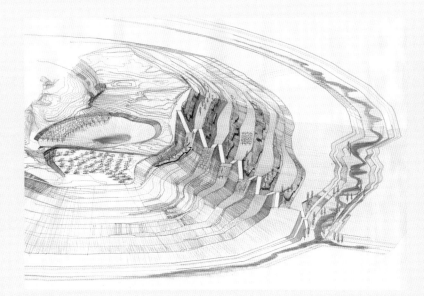

Above
Peter Latz's system of terraces is designed to manage water while creating a variety of settings for different activities and ways of moving through the site. Within this structure of terraces, the Ayalon stream will become a wide wadi that winds through and alters the riverbed to form lakes and ponds.

Angel with local architects Ulrik Plesner, David Guggenheim and Moti Kaplan, began working to secure the site and define its overall program in the form of a statutory plan. A team of scientists led by Danny Sternberg, who is now the park administrator, began to address the technical aspects of closing the dump.

Before I entered private practice, I was Central Park's chief landscape architect, and Dr. Weyl felt that my twelve-year immersion in the design, politics and public/private financing and management of Central Park's rejuvenation would be a valuable and parallel perspective to inform the planning process. Like Central Park, Ayalon Park will be an expression of the restorative capacity of landscape architecture and a symbol for its city.

From the outset, at the initial design workshop organized by Dr. Weyl and architect, Zurit Oron in February 2001, there was debate surrounding the design idiom for the park –would it have the naturalistic lakes and lawns of Central Park, or would the design be a response to the Mediterranean tradition of geometrical motifs and parsimonious use of water. Israeli landscape architect, Shlomo Aronson whose work though modern, fits seamlessly into the Israeli terrain, insisted that the park be realistic about water consumption, and suggested that the design draw from the language of agriculture. German landscape architect, Peter Latz, known for his work reclaiming former industrial sites emphasized the need for the park to have its own design

language that emerges from the systems and processes occurring on the site. And conceptual artist, Mierle Ukeles, who has committed a career to the subject of garbage, sees the act of reclamation as a symbolic of the human need to heal and regenerate. Niall Kirkwood, now the chair of Harvard's Department of Landscape Architecture, spoke of the park as a series of processes that occur over time, some short term, others long term.

After the workshop had posed questions of the park's significance for Tel Aviv, its content, appearance and management, it then begged the question of how to move towards a physical plan. It was decided to hold a design charrette to focus and elaborate on the park's planning and design, which I was asked to facilitate with Niall Kirkwood in January 2003. We expanded the knowledge base of the planning workshop by inviting international and local ecologists (Harvard professor Robert France, an expert in the restoration of contaminated sites, particularly water bodies, and Steven Handel who has been working on the landfill in Staten Island near New York) and landscape architects (Julie Bargmann, one of the United States' leading landscape architects in the restoration of disturbed landscapes, Ken Smith, known for his strong conceptual designs, Mario Schjetnan, known for the extremely large parks that he has completed in Mexico and Ellissa Rosenberg, a US leader in urban infrastructure). In all there were forty participants organized in groups to focus on four main aspects of the park design: the remediation of Hiriya; the design of the water system and related habitats, the arrival and movement of people through the park, and the question of how the park will be an expression of culture, image and society. We promoted an atmosphere of interaction and spontaneity by encouraging people to move among groups and by inviting mayors of the surrounding towns to respond to the work and tell us about their diverse constituents and ideas for the park.

A wealth of ideas emerged, many of which overlapped or complimented each other and were synthesized into a common vision for the park: Monumental and ritualistic, Hiriya will stand as a symbol of regeneration, looking out over a landscape of floodplains that, through terracing, will be transformed into uplands for intensive park use and wild lowlands for hiking and flood management. The lowland water system will be designed to handle both drought and flood conditions. The Ayalon Valley will contain reservoirs, wetlands, and wadis to store, filter and release water, allowing the system to accommodate a 10-25 year flood.

The higher ground to the north will become a more intensively used urban terrace, with playgrounds, small ponds and fountains, and other facilities to serve the

URBAN WILDS	PARK FIELDS	URBAN TERRACE
WATER RESERVOIR	SPORT FIELDS	"PASEO/RAMBLAS"
	FESTIVAL GROUNDS	
	ORCHARDS ORANGE	COMMUNITY ACTIVITIES
MEANDER STREAM	OLIVE	SMALL / INTERMEDIATE SCALE
WATER BIOFILTRATION WETLANDS	PALM	PICNIC
IRRIGATION RESERVOIR	AGRICALTURAL SCALE	BARBEQUE
		AMUSEMENTS
		GROVES
		ORNAMENTALS
		PERGOLAS
		GARDENS
NATURE SCALE	AGRICULTURAL SCALE	GARDEN SCALE

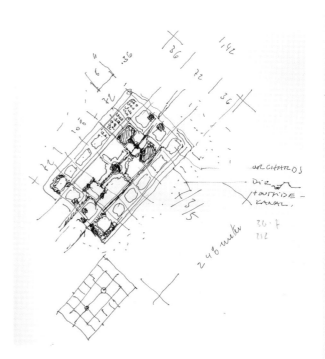

This page
In Ken Smith's Terrace Park, the site's uplands will be used most
intensively while the lowlands will be left wild for hiking and flood management The middle stratum ? a wide swath of agricultural floodplain ? can be used for activities requiring large open spaces, such as field sports and festivals.

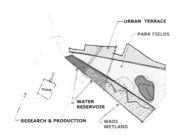

URBAN TERRACE
PARK FIELDS
WATER RESERVOIR
RESEARCH & PRODUCTION
WADI WETLAND

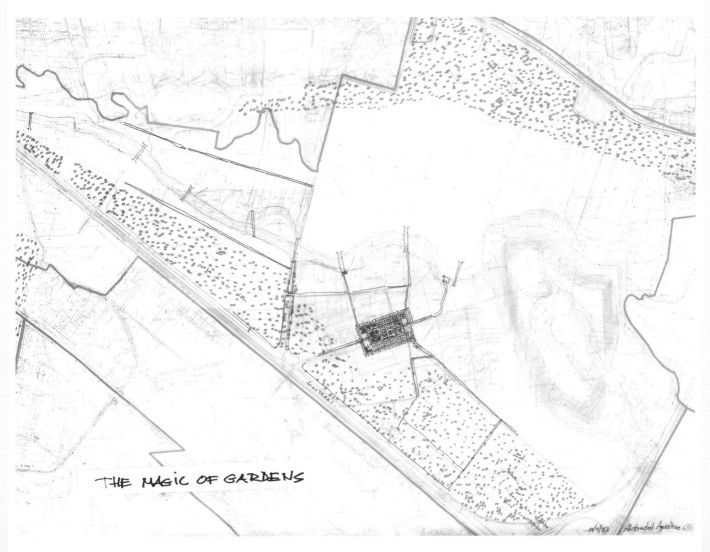

THE MAGIC OF GARDENS

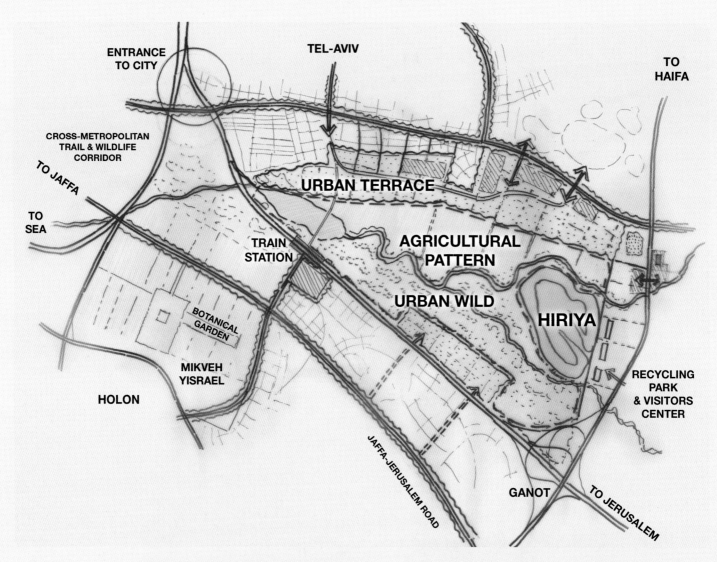

Above
Collective Ideas: Facilitators
Niall Kirkwood and Laura
Starr distilled overlapping
ideas into a diagram that
describes points on which all
forty participants agree. This
diagram can be used as a
framework for future park
development. (Illustration by
Ken Smith)

abutting residential communities. On this northern edge the park will have a relatively porous boundary, with multiple entrances aligned with local streets, small parking lots, and a connection to the Safari park that adjoins the park to the north.

Between these extremes the land will remain agricultural, or will be hold ball fields and other uses that require large tracts of lands. Much of the site will remain agricultural, as farming is both an expression of Israeli culture and an example of a sustainable landscape. The Mikveh Yisreal School, the country's first agricultural high school, will be restructured to help with park stewardship, and to provide agricultural programs related to the park's ecological systems. The school's grounds, which currently make up one third of the 2000-acre site, will become part of the park and, along with land currently being rented to farmers, will comprise the agricultural land supported by the fertile floodplain.

This conceptualization of the park as a series of terraces, or elevations, not only responds to the site's unique hydrology, but also creates opportunities for a grade-separated circulation system. Various ways of moving through the park - on foot, on bike, or on horse - can be accommodated without conflict.

The social ambition of the park as a place of interaction, where sub-cultures and groups can both stake out territory and mix, not only shapes the physical design of the terraces and paths but also drives very act of the park's development. In order to claim the land from its many owners and free it from other development pressures will require a broad based organization of varied social and economic parties. What will enable the park's implementation will be the continued refinement of the design into a vision so compelling that it will attract funding from an array of international sponsors, and will galvanize the political forces to promote its success. The extreme environmental conditions in Ayalon Park demand the creation of a landscape architectural language to redefine the idea of the public park for the post industrial era. ⚏

The New Slum Urbanism

of Caracas, Invasions and Settlements, Colonialism, Democracy, Capitalism and Devil Worship

The common usage of brownfield referring to a site first abandoned through disuse and then left fallow because of contamination, pertains to so-called Western, but perhaps more precisely Northern, post-industrial economies with shrinking populations and urban centres made obsolete through car-driven sprawl. In this context, a persistent brownfield stands apart as 'other' to the spatial order of the city. A redeveloped brownfield becomes a player in the larger social setting and environment. In the regions of the world where cities of 10 million or more continue to grow at an enormous rate, or where industry booms, the strategies and even the definitions of brownfield change. **Carlos Brillembourg** describes how such extreme sites and those who inhabit them shape the spatial structure of the Venezuelan capital, Caracas.

Jorge Luis Borges was asked, 'What do you think of improvisation?' He replied, 'Well, improvisation is very dangerous – it usually leads to vanity.'[1]

Over 400 Years of Invasions and Settlements
For about 130 years, from the time of Christopher Columbus until the conquest of Barbados in 1625, the Spanish monarchy governed North, Central and South America with the single exception of Portuguese Brazil. During this conquest and colonisation of the New World, a square grid centred on a main plaza was systematically applied in urban settlements as the street pattern of choice. In this way it came to be a representation of the rule of the church and the state over the large existing populations of indigenous peoples. The city structure was thus a calibrated instrument capable of representing the wishes of the king and facilitating the violent transformation of a (for the most part) pre-literate, animistic society into a monotheistic Roman Catholic one under the absolute aegis of the king of Spain.

Although these urban parameters had clear antecedents that were secular, in this particular case they were transmitted by means of edicts.

The new urban centres then served to execute the mass conversions of the Amerindians to the Roman Catholic faith. Once the conquest was accomplished, a stable and relatively peaceful political system continued to prosper and develop for the next 300 years. During the 1700s and throughout the 1800s, the great urban centres of Lima, Cuzco, Antigua, Bogotá, Quito and Caracas were growing and thriving.

In Caracas the square grid was differentiated by use and proximity to the origin point. This origin point was the intersection of the two major streets, Norte-Sur and Este-Oeste; it was also the location of the cathedral's bell tower. The tower served as a beacon, similar to the minaret in the Andalusian cities of Spain, orienting the citizens towards the plaza. The grid was adjusted for a plaza that was smaller than the typical square block. From above, this read as a cross with the plaza in the centre within the larger square grid. The addresses were not by way of street names. Instead a nomenclature of corners was used. Thus, the address for the foreign ministry was 'between Principal and Monjas'. This system of nomenclature transformed the open nature of the grid into a closed system of information.

The new faith (ie Roman Catholicism) was the origin for this grid. Buildings that served the church occupied the entire east side of the plaza, and half of the south side, along with the Archbishop's Palace. The City Hall occupied the southwest corner. It is very important to differentiate between this colonial and ideological grid and the 'space-allocation'-type grid that would later come to be used in North America, for example for New York City. The colonial urban grid came with a specific typology of housing and monuments, yet was flexible enough to adapt to the inevitable change in use that arose with the mercantilism of the 19th century, managing to retain its urban tectonics until the 1940s.

Colonialism, Democracy, Capitalism
In the latter half of the 20th century the expansion of Caracas followed internationally established patterns of urban form. The initial street-based urban typology

Previous page
View of downtown Caracas, 2002, with slums and low-income housing projects in the foreground. Half the population lives in these ranchos, which exist on land that is topographically challenged.

Right
Caracas plan 1891, printed in London, showing the square grid of colonial authority at its origin point, and the nomenclature of addresses organised by the corners of the squares rather than streets.

Far right
Caracas plan 'Rohl' 1934 showing the grid as a calibrated instrument in the violent transformation of the landscape.

became confined to a historical centre, and with the introduction of modern technology came the expansion through the valley of Caracas of satellite neighbourhoods connected by means of a system of intra-urban highways. This transformation of the traditional city from one of 'red clay tile roofs' to a modern utopia of high-rise flat-top buildings interspersed among trees and fed by highways was celebrated by the administration of Pérez Jiménez (1948–58), whose ideological underpinnings espoused a new kind of positivism.

The private sector joined in the cultural transformation and this soon resulted in a tropical modern city. Major projects by foreign architects such as Oscar Niemeyer, Roberto Burle-Marx, Wallace Harrison and Gio Ponti continued to build on a modern architectural vanguard that was begun in the 1940s by the Venezuelan architects Carlos Guinand Sandoz, Luis Malausena, Cipriano Dominguez, Carlos Raul Villanueva, Martin Vegas, JM Galia, Moises Benacerraf and Graziano Gasparini.

An example of a major urban renewal project, El Silencio (1941–5) by Villanueva, undertaken by the Medina administration, set an example which, during the Pérez Jiménez regime, was to become the norm. Excellence in architecture was promoted by state-financed projects such as Villanueva's University City (1944–70), Burle-Marx's Parque del Este (1956–62) and the 23 de Enero Development by Villanueva with the Banco Obrero. The new public spaces of the city projected an image of progress that was shared by both the public and private sectors. And this belief in progress through modern technology and architecture continued throughout Venezuela's democratic regimes up to and including the administration of Carlos Andrés Pérez (1989–93).

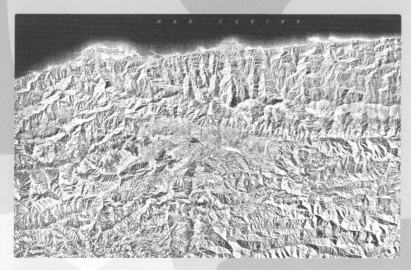

Top left
A religious procession in front of the St Teresa church. Through the traditional procession, the inhabitants traverse the ideological as well as physical boundaries of the colonial grid and the Modernist city.

Top right
Church of Petare (1700s) with slums in foreground. This contemporary self-built urban housing emerged as it became clear that the 1950s modern utopia was too expensive to build and difficult to regulate.

With the impeachment of Carlos Andrés Pérez came a new dystopic view of society. In the words of the architect and writer Federico Vegas: 'The balance between the marginal and the center was broken, and the marginal jumped into the center, in politics, in culture, and of course in the city.'[2] Next, after the interim one-year administration of Rámon Velasquez (1993–4, a multiparty coalition led by Rafael Caldera (1994–9) pardoned Hugo Chávez from his jail sentence for leading a failed coup on 4 February 1992. The current Chávez administration, although elected by democratic means, continues to dismantle all the institutions of the state, establishing a de facto dictatorship, characterised by a demagogic nod, that claims to represent the poor yet has increased poverty by around 25 per cent since 1999.The 1950s modern utopia turns out to have been too expensive and too difficult to regulate, and it is not accidental that the intra-urban ranchos appear as a marginal phenomenon at the time of the Modern City. The ideological underpinnings of this contemporary view can be traced to devil worship that begins in the colonial era as a contradiction to the strong Catholic ideology of the ruling classes, and as an attempt to achieve some kind of justice.

Devil Worship

The contemporary self-built and urban housing system (ranchos) currently houses half the population of Caracas and exists on land that is topographically challenged. These sites begin around the edges on a natural element such as a dry creek or in terrain that cannot be used for urban or agricultural systems: unstable slopes, dried-up creeks, spaces in between highways and ravines. The horizontal car-based urbanism of the 1950s is replaced by a vertical pedestrian system that is adjacent to the highways or existing urban centres. Public space is minimised, and the major public circulation paths are stairs that continue at 45 degrees for hundreds of metres without any landings. The material of choice in these slums is the hollow clay tile within a reinforced concrete frame.

Throughout the ranchos there is widespread distribution of free electricity. Each household has a television (primarily for the viewing of soap operas and adverts), a small refrigerator and an electrical hot plate. There are open sewers and only sporadic access to running water. State-sponsored interventions with the addition of community centres and schools are for the most part insignificant.

The formal urban structure of this labyrinthine housing system represents the anti-state or, in religious terms, the traditional devil worship of the dispossessed classes. This 'poor-devil urbanism'

Above
View of slum entrance in downtown Caracas, 2002. The hollow clay tile on a concrete frame is the typical material structure of this housing. The larger urban structure is labyrinthine.

Notes
1 From Roberto Alifano, *Twenty-Four Conversations with Borges, Including a Selection of Poems: Interviews by Roberto Alifano, 1981–1983*, Publishers Group West (Berkeley, CA), 1984.
2 In a letter to the author.
3 Michael T Taussig, *The Devil and Commodity Fetishism in South America*, University of North Carolina Press (Chapel Hill), 1980, p 112.

that settles on the extreme terrain and eventually achieves a density that is efficient in terms of zoning. This new city is made of recycled material taken from the excesses of an inefficient and excessive capitalism that tends to tolerate these slums as long as they are confined to the peripheries. Currently the slum urbanism surrounding the city forms a new kind of *Ringstrasse* and threatens all the public spaces in the once fertile valley below. The *buhoneros* (street vendors) on the one hand and the organised circles of armed gangs on the other proceed to occupy and control what is left of the plazas and streets of the old city (the *res publica*).

The specificity of each rancho arises out of a simple juxtaposition of topography and typology that protects the individual family unit within an environment that is both degraded and hidden. Here is the sacred/secret code with which the poor protect themselves from an oppressively axial colonial urbanism. The anthropologist Michael T Taussig points out the active nature of the devil worship:

> Two secular images in the language of sorcery materialize its magical aura: sorcery is person-made, and it is 'filth'. Although invisible powers forming an indistinct hierarchy led by the devil are prominent, the emphasis in sorcery is on the creative will of persons. Sorcery is the *maleficio*, the evil made, or it is, dramatically and simply, the 'thing made,' the *cosa hecha*. It is not seen as fate or as an 'accident of God.' The soul of sorcery lies in the poisoned breast of envy, and its dominating motif is filth.[3]

In other words, it is not god-given but manufactured by the *curandero* in an active engagement with nature. The devil is called upon to revenge the injustice of the poor, and human-made filth is the medium for this sorcery. This poor-devil urbanism evolves from the initial agrarian model to a hyperdense urban accumulation of multistorey units built in reinforced concrete on precarious terrain.

There is nothing informal about this new city. Form follows the reversal of the colonial model towards an urban architecture of resistance and despair. The temporary nature of the settlements is contradicted by their permanence and growth. The visual environment is ignored. The squalid surroundings notwithstanding, beauty and status exist in commodity fetishism: the trainer, the watch, the gun or the skateboard – all things that are lightweight and portable. The inhabitation of extreme sites by means of the new slum urbanism will continue to happen because this recycling of resources for the building of new slums in a benevolent climate is as natural a development for the developing world as the suburbs are for the developed world. ∆

creates the optimum amount of barriers to effectively shut out the state and the ruling classes. Animism is widespread. There is a culture of magic – *curanderos*, or shamans, taken from rural societies, become the arbiters of the community. The police will not enter, there are no doctors, no schools, the drug lord rules with a gun and the culture of violence is supreme. Gangs are the normative force. And fear is king.

The visual environment is also reflective of this condition which is now known as the poverty trap. The system does not permit gentrification. The military camp serves as the clearest architectural precedent. The individual family unit of the rancho is the tectonic brick

The Refugee Camp:

Ecological Disaster of Today, Metropolis of Tomorrow

Karl Ganser, the prime author of the Emscher Park Building Exhibition (IBA Emscher), has described how he finds suburban settlement patterns a more insidious form of brownfield than disused industrial sites. Mobility has replaced industry as the great agent of contamination. This project deals with a very specific and extreme form of mobility, namely forced migration. As in more normative cases, human mobility does not translate into ephemeral or temporary consequences for the environment. In fact, refugee camps are often lasting and urban in denotative terms of infrastructure, density and morphology. **Deborah Gans** and **Matthew Jelacic** present them as an enormous challenge and opportunity in themselves, and as an extreme lens through which to re-examine conditions of the everyday.

Refugee camps are a form of brownfield. They have physical impacts at the environmental and bioregional level so profound that the United Nations High Commission on Refugees (UNHCR) describes them as 'eco-disasters'. The problems include deforestation as refugees collect fuel wood and building material, consequent soil erosion and loss of biodiversity, poaching of wildlife, overcultivation of soil, water depletion, soil and water contamination from waste, air pollution from cooking fires and the production of vast amounts of garbage including shipping and construction materials.

The environmental policies now emerging to control the impact of the camps describes a planning vision almost Vitruvian in its combination of quasi-military techniques and ideality. Sophisticated satellite mapping and imaging of the geography can determine sites to accommodate settlements of 20,000 people with minimal environmental damage. The rule of thumb is a 15-kilometre-radius buffer zone between camp sites and natural areas to be protected, based on the circumference of the refugees' search for fuel.

Within the camp, the principle of forestation continues in the rule of 'no clear felling' of trees and shrubs throughout the site, and in the demarcation of additional areas of dense protected growth.

To accommodate the need for agricultural land within the maintenance of 'biomass', planners have developed systems like *taungya*, in which crops are planted between trees. Site-planning principles take into account environmental issues like erosion through simple measures such as running roads across, rather than up and down, slopes. Recommended plot sizes are quite large at a minimum of 400 square metres per household in order to encourage management responsibility of the immediate site and the addition of biomass through household planting. The cluster of four to six shelters around a shared central space is the favoured device of balance between the social benefit of eating and preparing meals within the family unit and the environmental advantage of collective cooking. Collective facilities such as markets and infirmaries are distributed according to criteria of walking distance and room for expansion.

In sum, the emergent planning principles of ecofriendly refugee camps bear an uncanny resemblance to enlightened urbanisms such as the New Bombay of Charles Correa or the Majorca Technopolis of Richard Rogers that challenge the culture of the car with the pedestrian radius of travel as the basic module for planning, reformulate the Modernist garden-city tradition as a productive landscape and envision an equitable society founded on equal dwelling plots. The difference between camp and city resides not in its temporary status but in its suspension of its residents' rights of self-determination.

These refugee camps, which are tantamount to cities without citizens, could well become the legitimised cities of tomorrow. The evidence lies in the colonial settlements and forced displacements of previous centuries that have become the metropoli of today. The trading companies of Europe considered themselves temporary occupants of undeveloped territories and focused on the extraction of wealth without the long-term investment of city building. They did not intend their forts, residential cantonments and roads as foundational plans for the exponential growth of the sprawling contemporary cities of Madras or Calcutta. The African cities of Ibadan, Nigeria, second in size only to Lagos, or Mbuji-Mbayi, the third largest city of former Zaire, originated in the displacements of population as a result of wars among indigenous as well as European empires.

IBADAN, NIGERIA

Ibadan began as a refugee camp in 1829 for the inhabitants of its antecedent city Eba Odan (literally, 'city situated near a grove'), which in turn had been founded in the 18th century as a colonial outpost of Yorubu warriors from Ife. As typical of their urbanising and colonising practices, the Yorubu spread to the region of Eba Odan, absorbing the indigenous population into their administrative reach as they established and extended the long-distance trade routes. One consequence of the battles among the various Yoruba kingdoms for control of territory was the actual physical displacement of Eba Odan's population to a camp site. Now more simply called Ebadan, as if to trace the loss of its original grove with the corruption of its name, this remnant city expanded rapidly as it became a permanent settlement for the wandering soldiers of Ile-Ife, Ijebu and the Oyo. The amalgam of refugee soldiers then solidified the political and military eminence of their phoenix capital, now called Ibadan, with their control over trade routes from the interior to the coast.

From 1865 onwards, Ibadan has been the single most important city of Yorubuland. However, despite its size there is a controversy as to whether it is truly a city because of its dual structure, whereby its core is inhabited by local indigenous peoples who spend half the week in their surrounding villages. It remains as at its founding, a temporary settlement with some permanent physical characteristics. Ironically, the most stable urban presence are its contemporary international immigrants and a literate elite linked to the renowned University of Ibadan, established by the British in 1949.

Key
1 Contours of hillside
2 Market location
3 Yorubu City wall of 1858
4 University College 1948
5 Perimeter of Ibadan 2000
6 Ona River
7 Trade routes
8 Projected perimeter of Ibadan 2020

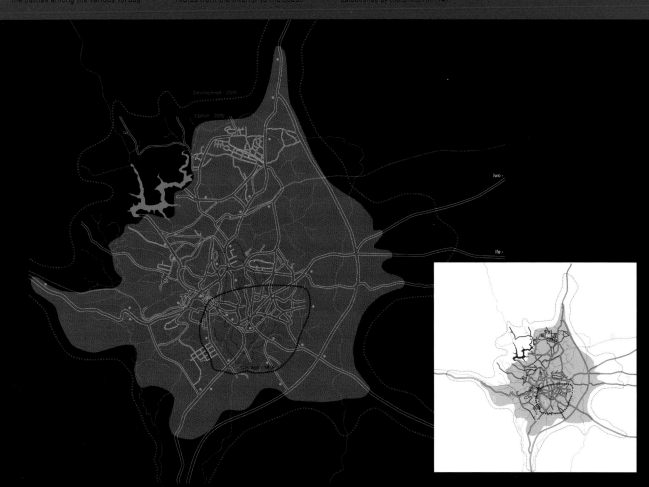

DADAAB, KENYA

Dadaab is a refugee camp on the Somalian border, established in 1992 in response first to the civil warfare and then to the natural disasters affecting the country. Its three compounds of Ifo, Dagahaley and Hagadera are currently home to over 300,000 refugees, most of whom have lived at the camp for over a decade. Prior to the establishment of the camp, the region of Dadaab was largely nomadic and pastoralist, with a permanent village population of less than 5,000. Today its local population is more than 10,000, many of whom have settled in relation to the wells, boreholes and other infrastructure of the refugee camps. These settlers are either former pastoralists attracted by the constant supply of water and food for their herds, or traders capitalising on the new market economy of the camps.

An anecdotal report describes how the indigenous settlements that have grown up around Hagadera remained when at one point the camp itself had been dismantled, like a ring of suburbs awaiting the rebirth of their host city. Hence the camp has been an agent in regional shifts from a nomadic herding towards an agrarian society and from an unsettled towards an urbanised landscape. The demographic and physical structure of Dadaab region is further blurred by the shared ethnic descent of the refugees and local population such that, while the refugees are officially confined to the fenced compounds and have no civic rights, there are Somalis of undefined origin living both in town and in camp. The familial reach of the refugees extends through the town and its immediate desolate landscape to Nairobi and Canada, where many of the refugees have been resettled, and it has instigated bus routes, trade connections and phone/communication networks across all of Kenya and beyond.

Key

1 Yorubu sultanic compound 1865
2 British fort 1924
3 Hagadera Camp 2000
4 Market
5 Greenbelt
6 Projected city 2020
7 Airport
8 Trade routes
9 Dadaab town 2000
10 Ifo camp 2000
11 Dagahaley camp 2000
12 River
13 Intermittent river

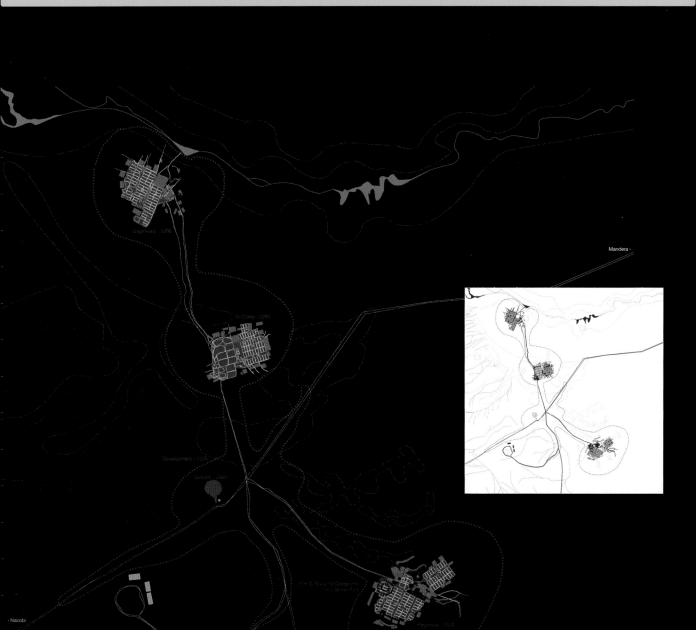

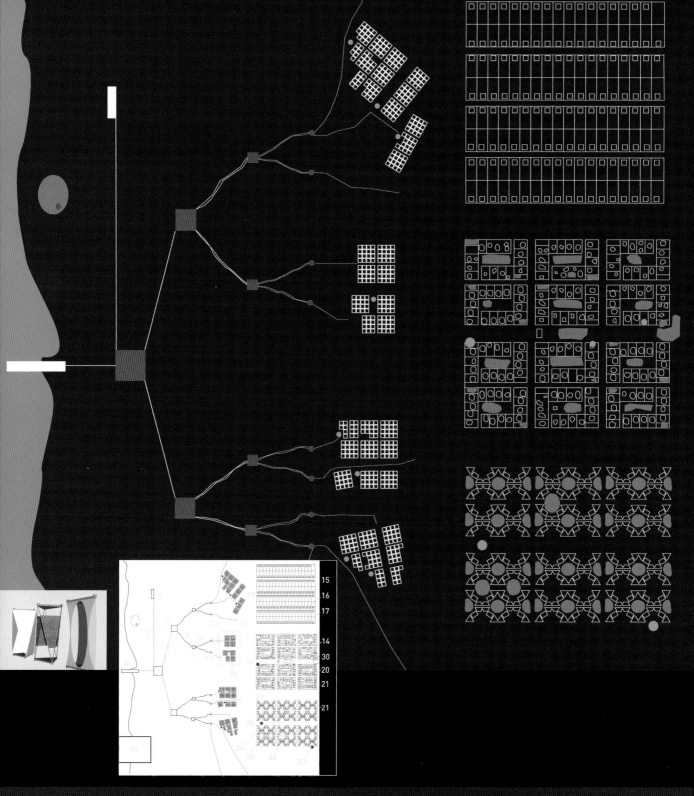

Refugee camp: components of a logistics system

While the host government has ultimate authority over the existence of a camp, the UNHCR often takes responsibility for its organisation and structure, much of which is standardised. The diagram is infrastructural, focused on the procurement, ordering, packaging, dispatch and delivery of goods as the foundation for the plan of the camp and the map of the larger landscape. Not surprisingly, the linguistic and physical logics of this refugee network bear a strong resemblance to military operations, especially in the period immediately following a disaster. As prospects of speedy return fade, the military character softens somewhat under the paths worn by quotidian events, the spontaneous assertion of customary patterns and the conscious cultivation of both literal and cultural nature on the barren site. The implementation of UNHCR ecoguidelines that prevent further degradation of the environment and encourage the grass-roots economic organisation of the refugees then becomes possible. However, the initially inscribed plan of a rigid grid with rows of tents precludes the radical spatial transformation of camps, and its trace will dominate the structure of the virtual city for decades after its reasons for being have faded.

Key

1 Capital city
2 UNHCR consignee field office
3 Airport
4 Port
5 Central warehouse
6 Long haul (up to 1,750 miles)
7 Regional warehouse and transport base
8 Medium haul (up to 175 miles)
9 District or local warehouse
10 Short haul (up to 60 miles)
11 In-settlement stores/distribution centres
12 Layout of large camp by UNHCR standards
13 Block for 1,000 people
14 Market
15 Block for 1,000 people of 600 x 600 feet by UNHCR standards
16 Family plot
17 Tent
18 Fire break
19 Block for 1,000 people after 10 years
20 Family compound
21 Mud or straw house
22 Greenbelt/vegetable garden
23 Local market
24 Regional market
25 Alternative configuration of block for 1,000 people with proposed shelter arranged in community clusters
26 Kitchen and cistern/shower
27 Privy
28 Living area
29 Protected community/play space
30 Greenbelt/vegetable garden
31 Illustration of kitchen and privy modules of proposed housing in a combination of high-tech (ceramic) and local (straw) materials

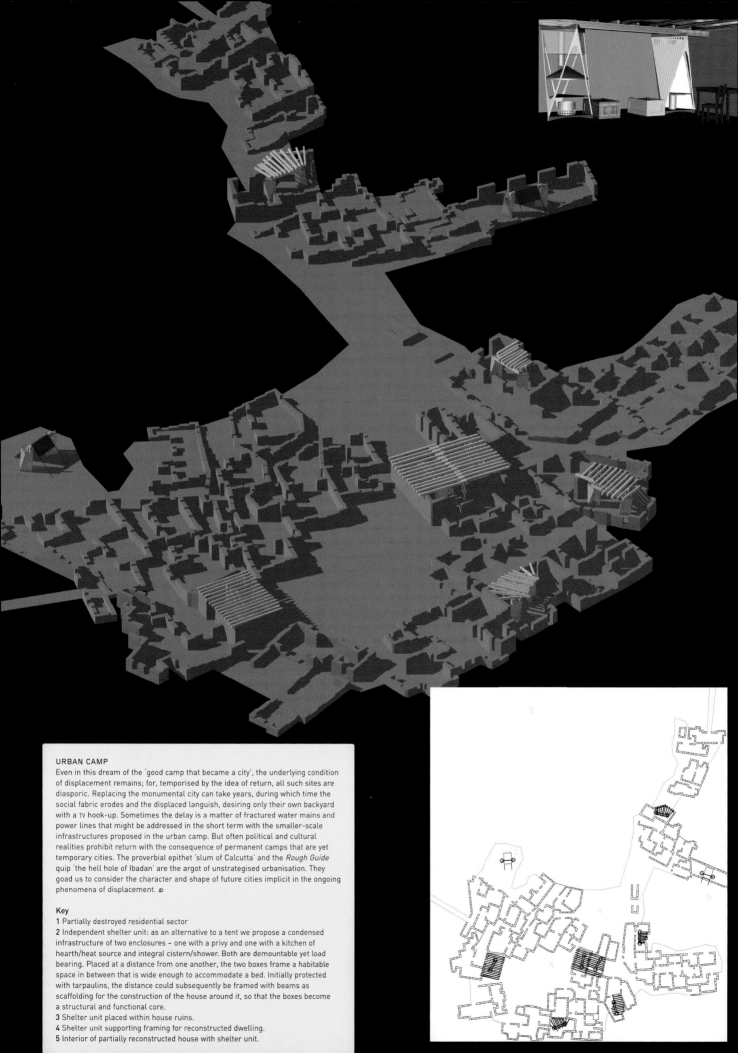

URBAN CAMP

Even in this dream of the 'good camp that became a city', the underlying condition of displacement remains; for, temporised by the idea of return, all such sites are diasporic. Replacing the monumental city can take years, during which time the social fabric erodes and the displaced languish, desiring only their own backyard with a TV hook-up. Sometimes the delay is a matter of fractured water mains and power lines that might be addressed in the short term with the smaller-scale infrastructures proposed in the urban camp. But often political and cultural realities prohibit return with the consequence of permanent camps that are yet temporary cities. The proverbial epithet 'slum of Calcutta' and the *Rough Guide* quip 'the hell hole of Ibadan' are the argot of unstrategised urbanisation. They goad us to consider the character and shape of future cities implicit in the ongoing phenomena of displacement. ₥

Key

1 Partially destroyed residential sector

2 Independent shelter unit: as an alternative to a tent we propose a condensed infrastructure of two enclosures – one with a privy and one with a kitchen of hearth/heat source and integral cistern/shower. Both are demountable yet load bearing. Placed at a distance from one another, the two boxes frame a habitable space in between that is wide enough to accommodate a bed. Initially protected with tarpaulins, the distance could subsequently be framed with beams as scaffolding for the construction of the house around it, so that the boxes become a structural and functional core.

3 Shelter unit placed within house ruins.

4 Shelter unit supporting framing for reconstructed dwelling.

5 Interior of partially reconstructed house with shelter unit.

Browning Maps

Brownfield is sometimes taken as the description of a *fait accompli*, the legacy of an industrial age that did not know better. These maps by **Deborah Gans** and **Denise Hoffman Brandt** depict the browning as an ongoing condition. Surely, on some level, we all understand that as long as we continue to drive more cars the steel to make those cars must come from somewhere. Even if we can recycle more and consume less, the search for raw material from water to coal to diamonds will continue. The mapping of these 'somewheres' reveals the workings of our current global economy, and simultaneously the situation of our global resources. Often they overlap in conflicting structures of threatened ecologies and natural payloads.

DAMS AND ARID LANDS

This map notates some of the social as well as environmental impacts of dams, challenging our visceral response to their illustrated physical grandeur and our conceptualisation of their great civic and infrastructural value.

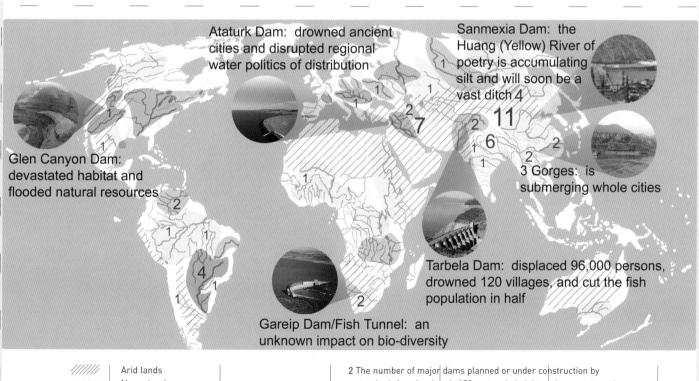

Ataturk Dam: drowned ancient cities and disrupted regional water politics of distribution

Sanmexia Dam: the Huang (Yellow) River of poetry is accumulating silt and will soon be a vast ditch 4

Glen Canyon Dam: devastated habitat and flooded natural resources

3 Gorges: is submerging whole cities

Tarbela Dam: displaced 96,000 persons, drowned 120 villages, and cut the fish population in half

Gareip Dam/Fish Tunnel: an unknown impact on bio-diversity

	Arid lands
	No major dams
	1 – 2 major dams
	3 – 6 major dams
	7 – 9 major dams
	10 – 14 major dams

2 The number of major dams planned or under construction by watershed. A major dam is 159 metres in height, or has a water volume of 15 million cubic metres in height, or has a reservoir storage capacity of at least 25 cubic kilometres. This count does not include more than 40,000 large dams worldwide, and up to 800,000 small dams.

GLOBAL RESOURCES

This overlay of sites with resources to mine and those with resources to be preserved makes the inherent environmental conflicts self-evident. In pairing threatened with honorific places, the map illustrates in the extreme a condition that is implicit in all the sites of development.

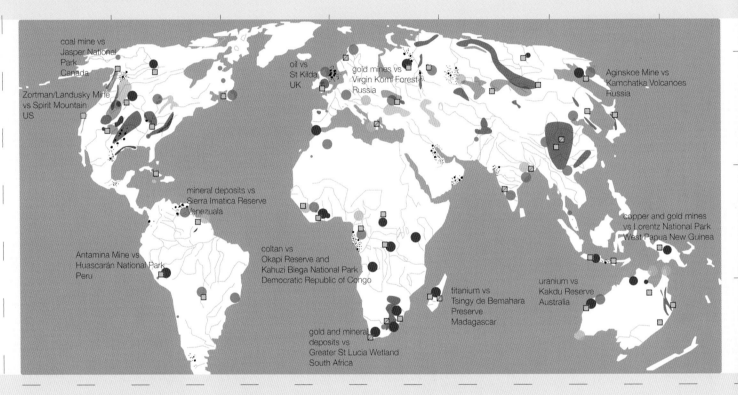

coal mine vs
Jasper National
Park
Canada

Zortman/Landusky Mine
vs Spirit Mountain
US

oil vs
St Kilda
UK

gold mines vs
Virgin Komi Forest
Russia

Aginskoe Mine vs
Kamchatka Volcanoes
Russia

mineral deposits vs
Sierra Imatica Reserve
Venezuala

copper and gold mines
vs Lorentz National Park
West Papua New Guinea

Antamina Mine vs
Huascarán National Park
Peru

coltan vs
Okapi Reserve and
Kahuzi Biega National Park
Democratic Republic of Congo

titanium vs
Tsingy de Bemahara
Preserve
Madagascar

uranium vs
Kakdu Reserve
Australia

gold and mineral
deposits vs
Greater St Lucia Wetland
South Africa

Global resources: deposits to be mined versus nature and culture to be preserved

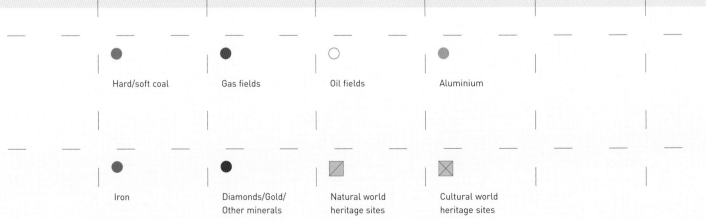

Hard/soft coal

Gas fields

Oil fields

Aluminium

Iron

Diamonds/Gold/
Other minerals

Natural world
heritage sites

Cultural world
heritage sites

TOXIC SITES

This map traces products of our industries of agriculture and mining that infiltrate the environment through water. Whereas the physical presence or absence of water is the measure of a dam, in the case of ground-water contamination the measure is nature's path of flow.

Various American and Canadian mining companies propose to expand operations in Colorado, Montana and Idaho which threaten to leach billions of gallons of cyanide effluent into groundwater

A Romanian/Australian joint venture spreads cyanide pollution throughout the Danube basin

The Aral Sea is a toxic desert

Cyanide: Summitville Goldmine -- $150M Clean-up

Residents ask to be relocated after cyanide-laced waste contaminates the River Asuman

Kelian Gold Mine contaminates the Kelian River

A Canadian company releases 24 million cubic meters of cyanide effluent into the Essequibo River

Toxic sites transcend borders

Mercury airborne and waterborne, a by-product of coal-burning power plants and small-scale mining operations.

Nitrate's high-pollution agriculture leaches nitrates into ground and surface water; high nitrate levels are associated with blue-baby syndrome and stomach and gastrointestinal cancers.

Cyanide used in mining operations to separate metal from ore; cyanide-laced water is stored at mine sites for reuse and leaches into the ground water or spills into surface streams. Arrows indicate international financing behind a few cyanide-contaminated sites.

Tenting on Terra Nullius:

The Work of Glen Murcutt

In his awe before the immensity and fragility of the Australian landscape, Glen Murcutt throws the entirety of its European development into question. Any permanent mark is a potential scar, any building site an eventual brownfield. He is fond of quoting Thoreau's passage on how man is a prisoner of his house, and of carefully describing the ventilation patterns allowed by the movable layers of bark cladding an Aboriginal hut. Yet, he insists, 'I am not rejecting urbanisation, far from it. I am not seeking a kind of utopia in the bush. I am involved with and recognise the importance of a varied milieu. I am opposed to the total taming of this land, my country, and the loss of the wilderness of the native scene.'[1] **Amy Lelyveld** describes Murcutt's search in European colonial thought and Aboriginal traditions for what he calls an architecture of 'refuge and prospect'.[2]

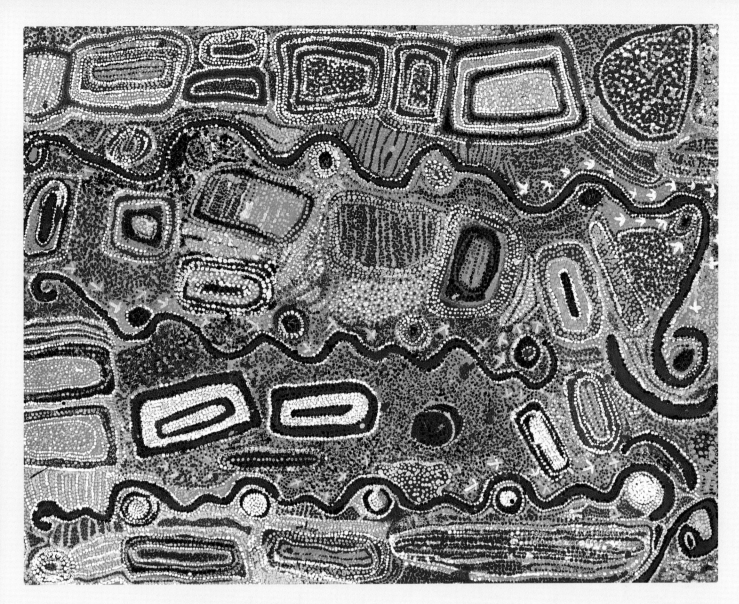

Opposite
Ball-Eastaway House, Glenorie, New South Wales, 1983. A Murcutt building in the bush – crisp, delicate, *en pointe*.

Above
Wimminji Tjapangarti, *The artist's country*, 1989. This painting asserts the artist's connection to his ancestral landscape. It describes a highly specific place complete with hills, creeks and water holes, and the tracks of a bird-footed ancestor.

A Murcutt building in the Australian bush – crisp, delicate, *en pointe* – looks like cutting-edge contemporary architecture. But it's more. For him it's a homily about place and propriety and a manifesto about how to build with honour on his continent. If you take a step further back you can read this light-footed creation as the result of a dance of two cultures – a hope-filled by-product of over 200 years of interaction between European settlers and a most ancient new world. Unmistakably, it's a vision forged by the evangelical power and pull of a sacred land.

In 1770 Captain James Cook arrived on the southeastern coast of what we know today as Australia and declared it '*terra nullius*' – or empty land. It had inhabitants, but he could not see any evidence that they used their land. They did not, for instance, till or cultivate it. Invisible to him was a different form of habitation – the dense weave of associations, songs and philosophy that bound as one not only the land but everything on it. The people were intimate with this land. Their songs caressed every inch of it. They mapped, explained, incanted, celebrated and protected it as kin. No, the land was not owned, it was embraced.

They spoke many different languages. They belonged to many different clans. They followed different customs. But the indigenous people of this ancient place that Cook labelled as 'new' shared a common concept of the Dreaming.[3] The Dreaming is certainly a people's story of their world's creation. But this intricate and mathematically elegant way of structuring society and man's place in nature goes far beyond creation myth. It is a people's historical record, system of living law and storehouse of knowledge of what is on the land and how to maintain it.

The Dreaming speaks of the time when the ancestors of every living thing awoke and created other beings in their image. They then proceeded to travel, shaping and naming their surroundings as they moved through them. As they sang the names of rocks, boulders, mountains and sinkholes they painted the profile of their world. Each ancestor travelled along an individual track. Between them their wanderings covered the earth – mapping it not in plots or parcels but with strings of song which, woven together, included everything. Their creation done, the ancestors returned to rest below the earth, leaving their descendants in the world.

Wombat, kangaroo, fish – each type of descendant formed a clan, inheriting an ancestor's dreaming and assuming the sacred stewardship of that ancestor's creation song and track. Even today, each child born is

rooted to a specific conception spot, which in turn binds the child to a dreaming track and the responsibilities towards, and knowledge of, the terrain it travels along.

The system created by the Dreaming was one that helped ensure survival both of the land and of those that lived upon it. Each individual within a nomadic community held an allegiance to, and knowledge of, a specific dreaming track. The combined information, when assembled, allowed a group to cast a net of intimate knowledge over a wide territory – essential given that the extreme and volatile environment necessitated a hunter-gatherer lifestyle. This strengthened the effective stewardship of a giving but fragile land, even as it made it impossible to delineate the kind of boundaries one could fence.

But none of this complexity was marked on the land. To the Western eye it was empty. Because it bore no marks of possession, European settlers refused to acknowledge it was owned by anyone. They considered the land ripe for the taking – a winning lottery ticket for a landless people who had no access to property, or the rights it brought with it, back home. As settlers arrived, there was more than enough of this boundless, unclaimed land to go around. Property was a leveller. Ownership transformed the settlers' place in society.

The land itself changed the settlers, too. It was unlike anything at home. The scale of the territory was truly vast. It was remote from every place else. It was also unnervingly different. Even in the present day, Australia has been described as:

… a world of such radical strangeness that it makes man lose all relevance – here man is completely superfluous. The true face of Australia is the face of the earth before the emergence of man, and it is also the face which earth will present again when man shall be no more.[4]

The land bore little resemblance to the farmland of Europe. So ancient that it is, in fact, geologically the oldest place on earth, it is also poor – having been unaffected by the ice ages or their fertile deposits. And because the climate is characterised only by unpredictable droughts and flooding, this poor land is fragile too. It is an extreme place where life in all its forms has adapted to the difficult and mercurial nature of its environment – or has done so temporarily, for everywhere is the sense that these finely wrought adaptations could be shattered.

Europeans tried to fence and remake this 'weird unawakened country'.[5] But Australia and its original inhabitants also to some extent remade them. Tendencies to travel and to live a spare life outdoors even under extreme conditions, have become fundamental traits associated with the Australian character.

Consciously and unconsciously, Glenn Murcutt has been shaped by the culture and history of his country. It is part of him. It is also fundamental to his work. In his buildings he creates his own hybrid – drawing on both the modern, Western architectural canon and the rich culture and powerful influence of the Australian land.

The workaday materials Murcutt typically uses in his buildings have a resonance in this 'most proletarian country'.[6] His corrugated metal siding and simple steel-pipe columns are the common hard-wearing and readily available materials used by Australian farmers in work sheds and shelters. He admires these farmers and their buildings where 'everything [is] cut down, stripped back'.[7] And his work celebrates their no-nonsense approach, led not by theory and aesthetics but by the demands of climate and landscape.

Murcutt's palette of common materials echoes simple settler structures. But it is when his architecture abstracts the imagery and conditions of the bush itself that one finds the deeper message of his buildings. Murcutt has described Australia's flora as:

... tough, ... durable, hardy and yet supremely delicate. It is so light at its edges that the connection with the sky vault is unsurpassed anywhere. The sunlight is so intense for much of the continent that it separates and isolates objects. The native trees read not so much as members of a series of interconnected elements but as groupings of isolated elements.[8]

The continent's intense sunlight tends to throw all things into a kind of crisp, even desiccated x-ray relief. This boniness has been recorded in Aboriginal paintings for thousands of years. On cliff faces or on bark, living things have often been presented without their padding. Emu, human, a school of fish – anything under the fierce Australian sun – is shown laced with what looks like decorative hatching. But what at first seems like pattern is really skeleton. Each being is shown filleted, internal organs exposed.

Murcutt's buildings, like the x-ray paintings, are whittled down to expose their skeletons. He strives for a spare and undressed architecture in which 'like a boat: every rib is necessary'.[9] He hones away until the systems of the building 'work in symbiosis and operate like muscles, sinews and bones'.[10]

This legible boniness, Murcutt says, reflects the way living things have adapted to the rigours of the Australian landscape:

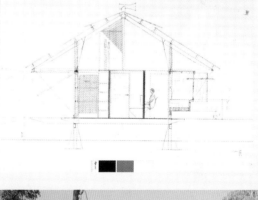

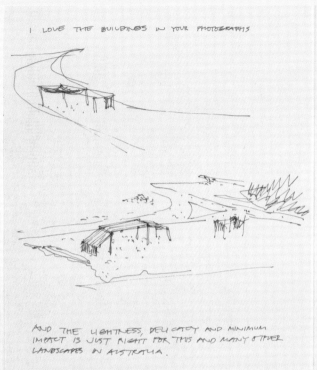

I LOVE THE BUILDINGS IN YOUR PHOTOGRAPHS

AND THE LIGHTNESS, DELICACY AND MINIMUM IMPACT IS JUST RIGHT FOR THIS AND MANY OTHER LANDSCAPES IN AUSTRALIA.

A tough landscape produces delicate flora: plants that grow in shallow leached soils, where rains intersperse with long periods of drought, develop in such a way that the leaves and branches feather towards their extremities. I was interested in how one can make buildings finer at the edges ... making building elements as light as possible.[11]

This mimicking of nature, as seen in his Magney and Marika-Alderton houses, is not just a matter of style but of ethics. On this fragile ancient land, minimalism and efficiency are imperative.

The fitting metaphor for Murcutt's architecture becomes a tent. 'What if I could make a whole building where it feels like one is living on the edge and can smell the rain and sense the changes in the air and light?'[12] Murcutt has mused describing his goals for the Marie Short House. The buildings are highly adaptable. Their lightness suggests that one is never really separated from nature:

I am not dealing with buildings with tight skins, where the joints have to be perfect. Many of my buildings have a loose-fit skin – like clothing, it's layered. Without air-conditioning and mechanical ventilation systems, the layers are removed or added according to climate, light levels, insects.[13]

Many of these structures are theoretically even movable. In the Marika-Alderton House not only is there no glass but it is built with:

All bolted joints. Nothing nailed. Everything screwed. The floor is screwed. This is very important for the future for if a material is screwed it is very easy to withdraw those screws and reuse it. I am using a lot of recycled timbers in the main sections. The whole building is bolted together.[14]

Elsewhere he describes the Ball-Eastaway House as 'a building that has docked, put out its bridge like a ship and is ready to go away'.[15] There's a built-in transience to these buildings that suggests they're about to move on – the other face of being so young and insignificant in such a very old place.

A linear Murcutt building in the bush runs with the contours of the land and tracks the movement of the sun. His buildings are not simply static extrusions. As you travel through them, the views change and their section modulates. Murcutt's buildings embody the idea of journeying through a landscape. They also suggest the deep culture of that landscape – the dreaming tracks and the journeys, both actual and in song, that keep the land alive.

Just as in indigenous Australian culture, there's a deep connection here between travel and refuge. This same duality of point and line can be found in the structure of the Australian landscape where it exists as the pull between one's own immutable bond to a conception site and the dreaming or ritual journey that

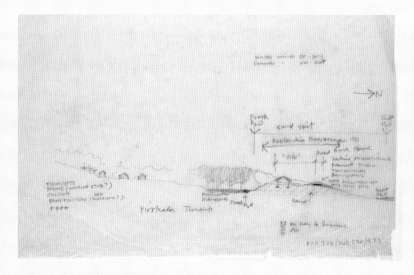

Notes
1 Glenn Murcutt, unpublished address, 'Some Old, Some New, and Some to Come', at the Yale School of Architecture, autumn 2002, when Murcutt was Visiting Bishop Professor of Architecture.
2 Ibid.
3 Andrew Sayers, *Oxford History of Art: Australian Art*, Oxford University Press (Oxford), 2001, p 18.
4 Simon Leys, 'Lawrence of Australia', *The New York Review of Books*, vol 4, no 8, April, 1994.
5 Leys quoting DH Lawrence.
6 Ibid.
7 Haig Beck and Jackie Cooper, *Glenn Murcutt: A Singular Architectural Practice*, The Images Publishing Group Pty Ltd (Victoria), 2002, p 63.
8 Murcutt, op cit.
9 Beck and Cooper, op cit, p 77.
10 Ibid, p 63.
11 Ibid, p 71.
12 Ibid, p 49.
13 Ibid, p 18.
14 Murcutt, op cit.
15 Beck and Cooper, op cit, p 71.
16 Murcutt, op cit.
17 Beck and Cooper, op cit, p 71.
18 Murcutt, op cit, quoting Lloyd Reese.
19 Murcutt, op cit.
20 Ian Jack, 'Introduction', *Granta the Magazine of New Writing, Australia: the New New World*, 70, summer 2000, p 8.

connects you to your ultimate source of your being.

Journeying is always rooted in a deep connection to one spot. This tenet of indigenous culture is Murcutt's mantra – or one of them. For him the essence and particularities of place are the code that guides his response to it. 'The very first drawing I do of any site apart from analysing all the other things is a section through the site to see where it's appropriate to build.'[16] Having identified that point in the landscape he works to develop a building that by its nature and character could be nowhere else. Like the first kick that binds a child in the womb to its conception site, for Murcutt this lock of idea to place is what determines both the nature and responsibilities of the building to be.

In Aboriginal culture the responsibilities of guardianship come with one's tie to a conception spot and dreaming. And with these ties come significant and intimate knowledge of place. Murcutt sites his buildings with precision to make the least intrusion he can upon the land:

For the final siting (of one house), the builder made a string profile of the plan, and four people held the corners to ensure all flora was retained and the support points in relation to the rock were appropriate. There was no destruction of plants.[17]

The buildings are articulated to bend in

deference to the character and rules of the site – the profiles of roofs are determined by sun angles, prevailing winds and the history of water on the site. Through these acts of preservation and observation a mechanism for understanding is created. A Murcutt building in the bush becomes a field station from which its inhabitants can take in the land. Each manipulation of their homes – each adjustment of a louvre, opening of a wall, each time they rise with the sun or track a full moon – binds them to the place.

In Murcutt's work we see the vision of an assimilated Australian – a European Australian made by the land.[18] It is a fundamental shift of view. To him the land – once thought of as empty – is saturated with structure and clearly dominant. The buildings upon it are tent-like and transient. They are built for the moment and momentary – for tracing time, light and weather – rather than posterity.

Some 220 years later, *terra nullius* is an absurdity. Australia's 20 million people crowd the periphery of the continent with cities and suburbs. Building takes place as it does almost everywhere, without regard for the fragility or traditions of the land. It is in this context that Glenn Murcutt is creating his subtle architectural synthesis, striking a delicate balance with the bush and staking an ethical position based on 'building out of our land'.[19] But this is not the general trend in that or any country. His position may not even be marked by the contemporary culture for which the canon and particularities of the bush may only have relevance as historic iconography.[20] For all its precision and place-based poetry, Murcutt's work is perhaps as invisible to the city-bound descendants of Captain Cook as the dreaming tracks were on the land dubbed *terra nullius*. Δ

Carlos Brillembourg is principal of Carlos Brillembourg Architects in New York. His built work includes a theatre, sports centre, office buildings, apartment buildings, a 250-room hotel, single-family residences and art galleries. He has received awards such as 40 Under 40, and was a founding member of the Instituto de Arquitectura Urbana in Caracas. He is the contributing editor for architecture for *BOMB* magazine, and editor of *Latin American Architecture 1929–1960: Contemporary Reflexions*, to be published by Monacelli Press in July 2004.

Ted Cavanagh and Alison Evans are faculty at Dalhousie University and principals of CoastalPlanners, a research design practice located on the Bay of Fundy, Nova Scotia. Many of their projects involve spatial design and planning, community-based technology and environmental management of the coast and ocean.

Deborah Gans is a partner at Gans & Jelacic Architects. The practice's current work in the area of displacement and transitional housing has recently been published in the 'Home Front' issue of *Architectural Design*, *Perspecta 34* and *Cities and Citizenlessness* (2004). Gans is co-editor (with Zehra Kuz) of *The Organic Approach* (Wiley/Academy, 2003), which is concerned with the interaction of environmental and digital technologies. She is an associate professor at the Pratt Institute and a critic at Yale University.

Denise Hoffman Brandt is a senior landscape architect at Mathews Nielsen Landscape Architects in New York. Her work focuses on the planning and design of public landscapes. She has received numerous design awards including a 1999 Visionary Landscapes Award from *Landscape Architecture* magazine and first prize in the international competition for Davids Island in New York. Her work has been exhibited at AIA San Francisco and the Van Alen Institute in New York. She is currently teaching at the Pratt Institute School of Architecture.

Matthew Jelacic is a partner at Gans & Jelacic Architects. The firm's current work in the area of displacement and transitional housing has recently been exhibited at the Slought Foundation and the Rosenbach Museum in Philadelphia. He is currently a Loeb Fellow at the Harvard Graduate School of Design where he is continuing research into the environmental and material aspects of displacement. He is a faculty member of the Pratt Institute and at the Parsons School of Design, the New School University.

Amy Lelyveld is principal of Amy Lelyveld Architect, New York, and a critic at Yale University where she has taught with Glenn Murcutt. She has won several AIA awards for her work as a designer at Miller/Hull Partnership, and has been widely published.

Himanshu Parikh is a director at Buro Happold, having merged his engineering practice in Ahmedabad with the firm. He is also a professor at the postgraduate School of Planning, Ahmedabad, visiting lecturer at the Department of Architecture, Cambridge University, and member of the Governing Council of the Department of Science and Technology, India. He has received several awards including the UN World Habitat Award in 1993, the UN Habitat Best Practice recognitions in 1996 and 1998, Aga Khan Award for Architecture in 1998 and a citation by the government of India for his pioneering work in slums.

Michael Sorkin is principal at the Michael Sorkin Studio in New York City. Recent projects include masterplanning in Hamburg and Schwerin, Germany, planning for a Palestinian capital in East Jerusalem, urban design in Leeds, UK, campus planning at the University of Chicago and a commission from the City of New York for a large park in Queens Plaza. Sorkin is the director of the Graduate Urban Design Program at the City College of New York. He is currently contributing editor at *Architectural Record* and *Metropolis*.

Laura Starr joined Saratoga Associates as a principal in 1997, after serving as chief of design for Central Park's Office of Capital Projects during the most active years of the park's reconstruction. Her leadership in park design, planning and management has been recognised nationally and internationally, most recently for Forest Park in St Louis, and in the organisation of international planning workshops for Ayalon Park in Tel Aviv.

Claire Weisz practises architecture and is the co-executive director of the Design Trust for Public Space in New York City. She has taught urban design at Columbia University and the Pratt Institute and has lectured about the firm's work and urban design. She has written articles on urban design and criticism for academic and Web publications, and her firm's work has been published in a number of books.

Mark Yoes graduated from Yale University and Rice University with degrees in fine arts and architecture. Articles about his work have been published in the *New Yorker*, *Architectural Record* and *L'Arca* among other publications and design books. He is a recipient of the Architecture League's Young Architects Award and has been finalist in a number of design competitions.

Peter Zlonicky is a planner, a distinguished visiting professor of planning at the Technical University of Hamburg and professor emeritus at Dortmund. He served as a scientific director of the IBA Emscher project. He has written widely on planning issues such as the auto-free city and continues to collaborate on planning projects throughout Europe.

Now Hear This

Below
Zankel Hall, an intimate new venue in the basement of Carnegie Hall, required
acoustic flexibility to host performances of classical piano, unamplified chamber
opera, world music and jazz.

With new concert halls debuting apace across the US, American architects are buzzing about the art and science of acoustics. **Craig Kellogg** listens in at a new auditorium designed by Polshek Partnership Architects – Zankel Hall in New York.

Stop the train: the soprano Renée Fleming is singing her solo in Zankel Hall. Would that someone could suddenly mute Manhattan's intrusive noises. Alas, Zankel is wedged into the basement of Carnegie Hall, cheek-by-jowl against the subway tracks. 'Nine feet away there's this several-hundred-ton thing going 50 miles an hour,' says one of Zankel's architects, Richard M Olcott, in only a slight overstatement of the situation. Resolving what Olcott, of Polshek Partnership Architects, told me was the 'very sensitive issue' of intruding subway noise occupied a great deal of his and his acoustician's time. In attempting to stop the transfer of vibrations from passing trains, the designers were careful to isolate as much of the basement's foundations as possible. However, work remains at the source of the noise, cushioning the subway tracks to muffle the rumbling where it starts.

Of course, taking such extraordinary pains makes sense in the design of new concert halls, where acoustics is a high-stakes game. A hall that performs poorly can expect enormous abuse over its life. Lincoln Center's flawed and dingy Avery Fisher Hall has started the New York Philharmonic Orchestra

publicly floating the idea of abandoning it altogether. Meanwhile, in Los Angeles Frank Gehry admits to having a happy cry in the balcony of Disney Hall months before it opened, upon hearing the first lonely strains played by a single violinist from the unfinished stage. Luckily for Frank, Disney Hall has been well received. In a radio interview, *The New York Times* critic Anthony Tommasini pronounced Disney's sound 'nice bright and modern', while still leaving himself a little wiggle room when he noted that 'a hall settles in as the paint dries'.

In print, Tommasini reported his initial reactions to Zankel as mixed: 'The sound seemed bright but not especially warm,' he wrote. 'Details and definition came through better at soft volumes, as when Ms Fleming accompanied by the pianist Emanuel Ax, performed Strauss's dreamy song "Morgan!", than at full volumes, as when the same artists gave an impassioned account of the stormy "Cäcilie".' But it is precisely such squishy and ultimately subjective pronouncements that set the parameters for acousticians. The process typically

Below left
The view from the stage includes movable, circular acoustic clouds overhead that
redirect sound which would otherwise diffuse among the lights and ceiling trusses.

Below right
Slatted sidewalls at stage level conceal QRDs, elements with narrow
wooden fins that diffuse sound with frightening efficiency.

starts with case studies of historic venues that have enjoyed
critical acclaim. Before the introduction of computers into
the design process, says Christopher Jaffe, of Jaffe Holden
Acoustics, new halls simply copied others that worked.

Today designs are tested with science, calculations. Early
in the development of Zankel Hall, Jaffe rejected the idea
of building an oval room. Working from what Olcott calls
a conceptual schematic design also led Jaffe to another
conclusion with startling – and expensive – implications.
To produce the necessary reverberations for 'clarity' that
was not harsh (too little reverb can sound harsh), the volume
of space under Carnegie Hall would have to be doubled.
Ultimately, this required excavating an additional 8 to 12 feet
of rock from the floor of the basement.

Jaffe designed Zankel with a lower reverberation time –
less echo – than a bigger, symphony hall. 'We wanted enough
reverberation for a roundness of tone, but didn't want the
sound to linger to the point that it would get muddy.' He terms
this 'definition' with 'warmth'. Jaffe encouraged a little more
of the low frequencies than mid ones, to allow the warmth of
cellos, violins on the G-string and lower woodwinds its due.

Despite the added volume, Zankel is still relatively small at
680 seats – a number far less than the 1,000 the Carnegie Hall
brass would have preferred. However, the new room displays
spectacular flexibility to accommodate educational
programmes for schoolchildren on one hand, and jazz jams,

unamplified chamber operas or electrified world music
on the other. The floor rises or lowers in strips, each
mounted on a separate elevator. So the room can be
configured with patrons sitting on a series of gently
sloping terraces for traditional end-stage performances.
Alternatively, a square piece of floor rises at the centre
of the room for performances in the round. (Think of
musicians performing in a boxing ring.) For master
classes or to accommodate educational groups, the
entire floor can be flattened into a single plane.

Naturally, it goes without saying that such flexibility
requires nimble acoustic design. Unamplified musicians
in the end-stage configuration must be able to hear
themselves, for instance. In this case, the wooden wall
at the back of the stage also reflects sound to the
audience sitting on the rear terraces. For the centre-
stage layout, where the audience completely surrounds
the performers, a series of circular stretched fabric
'clouds' on aluminium frames drop from the ceiling at
the centre of the room, reflecting sound to the far ends.
Of course, pictures of the clouds have appeared in other
publications. But there is no guarantee you would ever
learn that they focus sound – nor that the volume of
the room affects reverberation time – if you hadn't
just read it here. Jaffe says, 'We're not always called
by the architectural press.' ∆

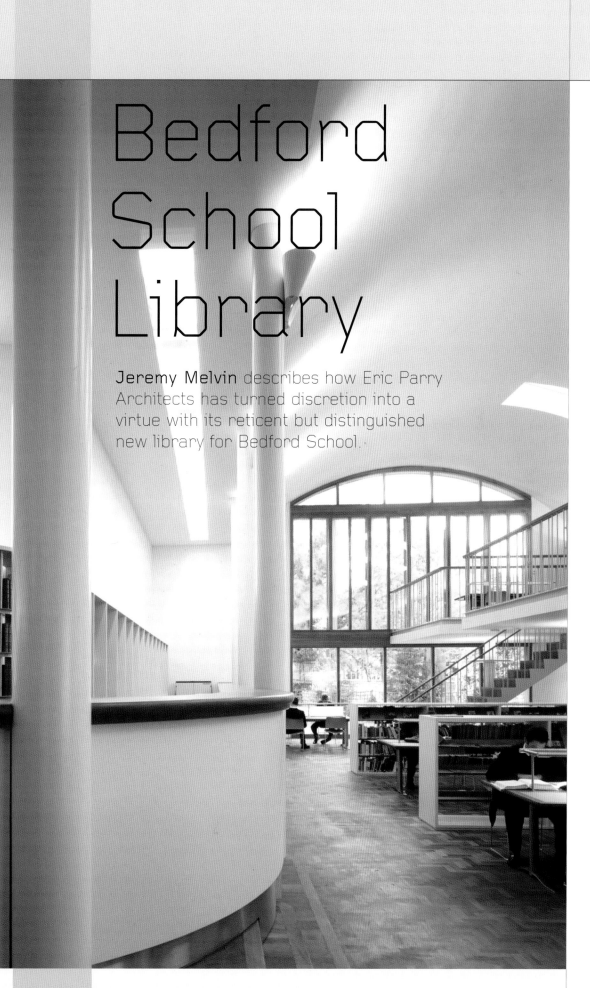

Bedford School Library

Jeremy Melvin describes how Eric Parry Architects has turned discretion into a virtue with its reticent but distinguished new library for Bedford School.

Previous page
The librarian's desk is positioned to supervise both the mezzanine
and main reading levels. The interior is unexpectedly light.

Below
Eliminating ties and secondary structural members, the underside
of the roof reads as a single organic form.

Inset
Conceptually the treatment of space, form and light brings
to the secular what was once reserved for sacred spaces.

Bottom
The roof form is made up of numerous different spans, each
following the overall form to give as smooth a finish as possible.

Some English public schools (that is, those which charge fees) have superb buildings, and others educate their pupils in whatever comes to hand, but most, if not all, take architecture for granted. Unlike in Athens, the English climate makes buildings unfortunate necessities to provide shelter for teachers to drill their charges with Latin declensions and German irregular verbs – inconvenient and occasionally expensive lumps of brick, stone or whatever which fill the spaces between rugby or lacrosse pitches. Like many of its counterparts Bedford School, an ancient foundation in the Midlands town of the same name, has a motley collection of buildings whose coherence is not helped by the flat landscape and weakly defined edges of its campus which leak into anonymous suburbia. But as the eyes become accustomed the buildings seem to take on a character.

Predominantly in a red brick whose clay comes from the local soil, a chapel and memorial hall by Oswald Milne, best known for the Art-Deco interiors of Claridge's hotel but here employing a sedate Arts and Crafts idiom, plus the great hall in the sort of 19th-century Gothic frequently found at small but distinguished

American colleges, stand out against ordinary houses and the ravages of 1980s design and build.

Among them, discreet and almost retiring at first sight, is the new library designed by Eric Parry Architects. Its apparent reticence springs from three conditions: much of its exterior comprises a continuous band of solid brickwork in the familiar reddish hue; its form seems to retreat into the background; and its site is not prominent. But on further acquaintance the design gradually assumes considerable presence and force, precisely because of the way it addresses and manipulates these three conditions. Using local brick immediately ties it to the background, but raising the band of brick above the ground gently inverts this relationship and reveals part of the interior, something none of its immediate neighbours do. In addition, giving the brick a subtle yet perceptible curve further removes it from its familiar role, and might take it close to Surrealism except that the curve bulges towards the most visible corner, drawing as much attention to itself

Top
Site plan. The new library
occupies a former car park on
the edge of the school's site near
the memorial hall. Eric Parry
Architects has also commenced
work on a new music school
alongside the chapel.

Middle left
Ground-floor plan. The canted
plan opens from the entrance
to the librarian's desk, which
naturally distributes visitors
to the computer terminals or
reading areas and has views
of the entire space, ground
and mezzanine levels.

Middle right
Cross-section. Aside from the
seminar room and ancillary
spaces, the complex, irregular
U-shape makes a single volume
though varying light and
form suggest subdivisions.

Bottom left
Mezzanine level. As well as the
reading gallery, there is a
seminar room on the upper floor.

Bottom right
Section through east elevation
(left). Making the curving wall
one brick thick makes it read as
a volume as well as a surface.
Sketch perspective (right).
Although virtually invisible from
the outside, the roof's complex
double curvature, irregular span
and carefully placed skylights are
essential to the internal effect.

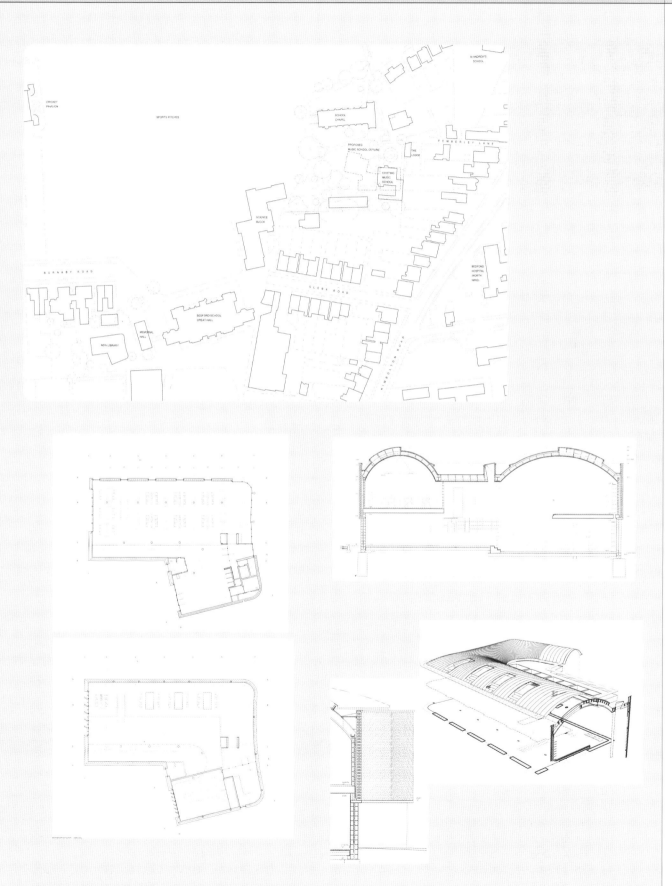

Below
Mixing the familiar with the uncanny, the
library brings intrigue to the school's campus.

as possible on its backland site. In an appropriate architectural analogy of the library's role within the school, its design manages simultaneously to intrigue from the outside while offering protection to the inside.

Recent architecture at the school is mixed. The most notable example is the rebuilding of the great hall by Philip Dowson of Arup Associates, after the hall was destroyed by arson in 1979. Constrained by the remaining shell and more or less invisible from the outside, its idiom might be termed 'glulam Gothic' – a brave attempt to interpret late-Victorian architecture using contemporary timber techniques. Its effect is not unlike Giles Gilbert Scott's rebuilding of the House of Commons after the Second World War bombing, and is wholly appropriate to the portraits of former headmasters which line the walls. Inevitably, though, there are design-and-build eyesores, and perhaps the realisation that procuring buildings in this way is not a universal panacea was one of the reasons behind the school's decision to bring design quality to the fore in the new library, calling in the RIBA to organise a competition.

However, probably a more important reason was the need for such schools to offer better and more varied experiences to their pupils, whose parents tend to have very high expectations for the return on their investment in their children's education.

Also to this end, the school has recently commissioned Eric Parry Architects to design a new music school on a site some distance from the library.

Probably the greatest challenge in designing a library is to strike an appropriate balance between civic presence and an intense interiority that encourages study. As described above, Parry's design does exude a power that seems to grow the more one looks at it, just as the glazed ground-level corner betrays its function. There is no doubt that this is both a library and an important building within the school precinct. But nothing on the outside gives away the atmosphere of the interior. What seems heavy from the outside is light, bright and airy within. And if the exterior curve is heavy and serious, as if wrought from a solid form, the interior is almost playful in its variety of form, shape and texture.

Only on the inside is the overall composition apparent. It comprises two wings of different lengths and widths, set at a slight angle to each other. This arrangement generates the slight concave curve, a form that naturally attracts people to the entrance and brings them, once inside, to the point where the wings meet – the librarian's desk, equally logically placed for

Below
Both the seminar room (pictured) and the reading area have powerful west windows.

Bottom left
The seminar room.

Bottom right
On the inside the intrigue is revealed and knowledge offered.

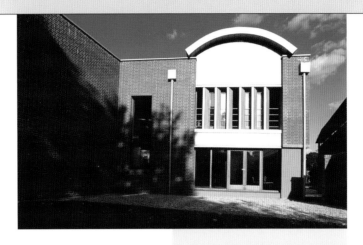

surveillance of all areas. In the shorter wing to the left are lockers and computer terminals, as well as a staircase leading to a seminar room above, while to the right the floor drops a few steps into the larger wing, which holds the main shelves and reading areas. What from the outside appears solid here becomes space, programmed and tuned for study. Light reverberates like music from rooflights in the barrel-vaulted roof, through the fine balustrade or down light-wells through the mezzanine to the ground floor.

There may be a delicate and oblique analogy with reading here: a book's cover can only intrigue and précis; only from the inside does its full meaning become apparent. But there is also a subliminal reference to church design, suggesting the old Enlightenment notion that learning should become the equivalent of religion in a secular society. The strip window on the entrance front establishes a visual relationship between the outside and the least intense internal activity, while the opposite end culminates in a grand window that modulates light across the principal reading areas.

As always with Parry, construction techniques are carefully crafted and deliberately chosen to reinforce the overall effect. The curving wall achieves its massiveness and presence partly because it is one brick thick, and laid in Flemish bond with lime mortar so that it avoids expansion joints. Consequently it reads as a taut, organic surface to a living form. But the constructional feature that holds the whole design together is the extraordinary roof. Not only does it have to double back on itself, it also has to adapt to varying spans and the concave curvature of the entrance wall. Within the mainstream tradition of English architecture such a feature would be expressed for its own merits, but for Parry, working with engineers Adams Kara Taylor, the effect is as important as the form of construction. What is extraordinary is that it is achieved without tie rods, with all lateral forces being carried in the walls, so the roof itself is almost a single skin covered in a standing-seam metal sheet and finished on the underside with extremely smooth plaster. More or less invisible from the outside, it is the smoothness of its internal finish that reinforces the sense of space and light of the interior.

In this small and subtle addition to its building stock, Bedford School has not only gained an important facility but has achieved a library of comparable quality to those of Oxford or Cambridge colleges – an aspiration that should not be lost on the pupils. ᴁ

How Green Is Your Garden?

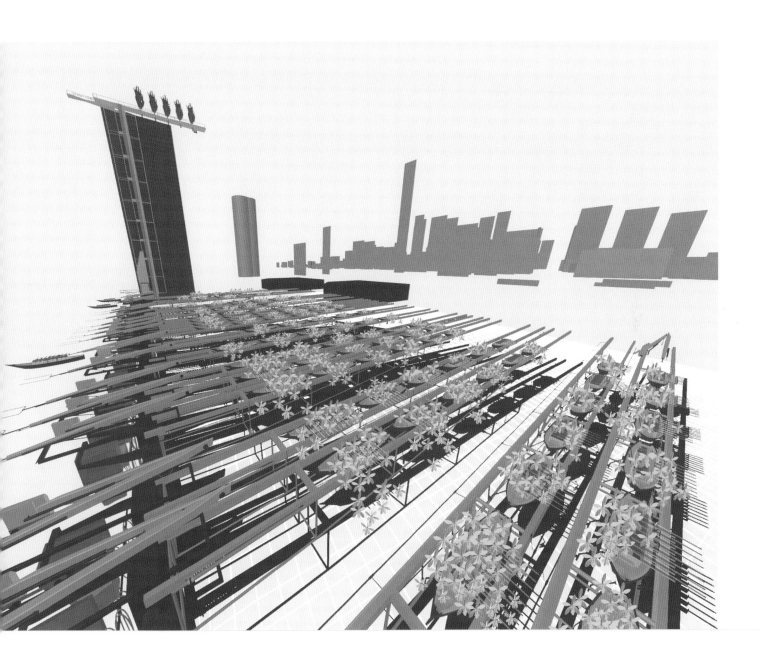

Follow the adventures of Alicia Liddell as she mounts an expedition through the uncharted landscape of the family Victorian flat, in *How Green Is Your Garden?* by CJ Lim. Peering from beneath our heroine's flights of fancy lie questions of an ecological bent, focusing on the impact of the environment on architecture rather than architecture on the environment. Is it possible for buildings to learn from organic systems? And can the banal interactions of flora and fauna in the domestic flat be scaled up into hybrids of growing edifices and engineered gardens of gargantuan size?

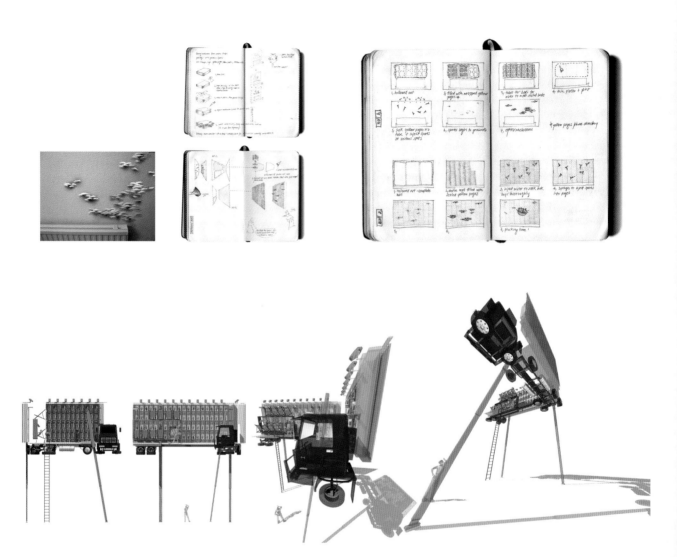

The new Liddell home could be described as quite minuscule. It was not the sort of place where a child could walk through a hidden door into an enchanted wonderland beyond or even discover long-forgotten treasure in a secret passageway. Alicia sorely missed life in the country where she had been allowed to cavort in the mud and rain. Here in the city, strange notions of urban decorum had prevailed over her parents; raincoats, umbrellas and staying inside had become the order of the day. It was with this thought that Alicia resolved to bring the countryside to 95 Greencroft Gardens.

She began projecting her jottings into plan form, circumscribing areas of light and dark, moist and dry, warm and cold with sure confident lines, feeling the bite of lead into vellum. All the while she rummaged through her botanical knowledge for plants that thrived in light and dark, dry and moist or cold and warm conditions. 'Mushrooms grow in dark moist areas,' noted Alicia, 'and can live on old coffee grounds. Moss can grow on virtually anything, and I know just the place to find some.'

Underneath her drawing, she wrote herself a list of things to do:

1. Grow a portable moss rug to carry from room to room to have indoor picnics.
2. Create miniature green worlds invisible to the naked eye (inspired by the Chinese ideal of cultivating a garden no larger than a mustard seed).
3. Plant a chive path around the rim of the bathtub.
4. Construct a strawberry chandelier so strawberries can be picked and eaten at the dinner table.
5. Grow a living coat from grass to wear.
6. Cultivate a corridor of mushrooms.

All good experiments begin with research, and Alicia did her homework on the best ways to grow mushrooms. Yes, mushrooms could grow on old coffee grounds, but the coffee-flavoured mushrooms did not really appeal to her. Word-flavoured

mushrooms, however, sounded more stimulating for both mind and body. Father had reacted quite hysterically when she had asked if she could borrow his books on classical architecture as a growth substrate for her mushrooms, but she had thought better of it anyhow as the mushrooms would probably not survive in such a dry environment. When he had calmed down somewhat, he did make the rather good suggestion of using the old phone directories sitting in the communal hall that none of the other residents had collected.

Next, Alicia had to decide on what type of mushrooms to grow. Redcaps, perhaps? The idea of eye-catching red mushrooms sounded like just the thing to enliven those dull white walls in the hall. She finally settled on *Pleurotus pulmonarius*. The idea of cultivating a hall of grey oysters rather appealed to her. When she passed through it every day, she would be able to conjure up walruses and other sea creatures in her mind's eye without the use of magic.

In case she wanted to repeat the experiment later and possibly improve on it, Alicia wrote down the following instructions in her notebook:

Take one phone book and soak thoroughly with water (rainwater is best). Wrap in plastic and shrink to fit with a hairdryer. Then, inject a few squirts of mushroom spores using a syringe to provide even coverage. Place in a dark, warm and damp environment and wait for the mushrooms to sprout.

To make the hall sprout with mushrooms, make a small opening in the wall and insert the prepared phone book into the hollow. Cover with mesh and a thin layer of plaster and paint to make indistinguishable from the surrounding area. Repeat as desired indiscriminately.

Alicia was particularly proud of this last bit. The only mitigating thing about how pig-headedly slowly plants and fungi grew, Alicia felt, was that her botanical misdemeanours would not be immediately apparent. This enabled her to defer and ration out her tellings-off so that they were at least bearable, and she considered the mushroom hall to be her most ingenious hidden-garden scheme. This was her *pièce de résistance*; for her parents it would be the final straw. ∆

CJ Lim is a director at the Bartlett School of Architecture and the Bartlett Architecture Research Lab. He is currently visiting professor at the Mackintosh School of Architecture. The first recipient of the RIBA award for academic contribution in architectural education in 1997, he received the same award again in 1998 and 1999. His publications include *441/10 ... We'll Reconfigure the Space When You're Ready* (1996), *Sins and Other Spatial Relatives* (2000), *Realms of Impossibility: Air* (2002), *Ground* (2002) and *Water* (2002).

If you enjoyed reading this article, then you might be interested in purchasing *How Green is Your Garden?* by CJ Lim, 208 pages PB (ISBN 0470845392), available to *AD* readers for an exclusive price of £ 14.99 (25 % off rrp). All you have to do is quote the code DBB when you order directly through John Wlley & Sons Ltd, and you will receive the book at the special price (+p&p).
Offer valid until end of June 2004. Order using any of the methods listed at the back of this issue or by visiting www.wileyeurope.com, ensuring that you quote the promotion code to take advantage of this offer.

Sergison Bates Architects

Advocating 'reduced form-making based on the familiar images of buildings', the London-based practice Sergison Bates Architects combines rigorous and conceptual material expression. **Lucy Bullivant** explores the consistency of this approach in the practice's recent housing and education schemes.

Sergison Bates is spurred on by a number of concerns that certain of its luminary elders, who prefer a promiscuity in expressiveness informed by a rich palette of materials, simply cannot relate to. The abiding strengths of the practice lie in its strategic use of a reductive language of material and construction in projects to date, predominantly in the public sector, such as housing and schools.

The firm's engagement with a larger scale of major urban framework design, as borne out by its work in collaboration with the urban-design practice East for the London Borough of Barking and Dagenham (following a 2002 competition), adds a further element in the professional arsenal that will serve Sergison Bates well in today's climate of committed urban regeneration.

Firstly, the architects 'seek an authenticity in construction where the nature and intensity of material is expressed directly and with rigour'. However, instead of being dogmatic about

how a structural solution can be achieved, they deliberately conceptualise construction, lending it the means to express the presence of a space. What matters is the feeling experienced by wood or masonry, albeit quite subliminally in some cases. This is very far from the classic UK high-tech position that relies on the fetishistic power of details.

'We need to be obsessed with construction in order to be loose about it and to make work that engages with what is there – with the real and the ordinary,' say the architects Stephen Bates and Jonathan Sergison. Accordingly, they make representations of the specific and universal conditions they observe, knowing that composition and spatial relationships can heighten ambiguity and also humour, just as can the seminal works of Minimal and Pop Art, for instance a work the practice admires, Bruce Naumann's 1983 *Dream*

Sergison Bates Architects Sergison Bates Architects Sergison Bates Architects Sergison Bates Architects Sergison Bates Architects Sergison Bates Architects Sergison Bates Architects Sergison Bates Architects Sergison Bat
n Bates Architects Sergison Bates Architects Sergison Bates Architects Sergison Bates Architects Sergison Bates Architects Sergison Bates Architects Sergison Bates Architects Sergison Bates Architects Sergison Bat
n Bates Architects Sergison Bates Architects Sergison Bates Architects Sergison Bates Architects Sergison Bates Architects Sergison Bates Architects Sergison Bates Architects Sergison Bates Architects Sergison Bat

Sergison Bates Architects, 'Classrooms of the Future', Bedfordshire, 2003
The project included Burgoyne Middle School, Maple Tree Lower School and Sandy Upper School, and was commissioned by Bedfordshire County Council in response to the £13 million 'Classrooms of the Future' initiative launched by the Department for Education and Skills (DfES) with the aim that design could promote educational advancement. Three low-lying buildings, they are envisaged as 'pieces of occupied landscape' and an appendage to each school which extends into a landscaped setting. Each building is a balloon frame with steel enhancement, with oversized standing-seam roof lanterns emerging from behind the roof plane, increasing the internal volume but also reflecting the roof forms of the adjoining buildings.

Burgoyne Middle School

Above and right
The new building for Burgoyne is intended as a facility for the whole school and for use as a community and research centre. It serves as the entrance to the school, offering views into the classrooms to visitors, and is clad with hardwood timber that expresses their relationship to the landscape and resembles a screen that wraps itself around the complex plan forms. It is detailed so that the layers of construction are clearly visible.

Bates Architects Sergison Bates Architects Sergison Bates Architects Sergison Bates Architects Sergison Bates Architects Sergison Bates Architects Sergison Bates Architects Sergison Bates Architects Sergison Bates Architects Sergison Bates Architects Sergison
Bates Architects Sergison Bates Architects Sergison Bates Architects Sergison Bates Architects Sergison Bates Architects Sergison Bates Architects Sergison Bates Architects Sergison Bates Architects Sergison Bates Architects Sergison Bates Architects Sergison
Bates Architects Sergison Bates Architects Sergison Bates Architects Sergison Bates Architects Sergison Bates Architects Sergison Bates Architects Sergison Bates Architects Sergison Gates Architects Sergison Bates Architects Sergison Bates Architects Sergison Bate
Bates Architects Sergison Bates Architects Sergison Bates Architects Sergison Bates Architects Sergison Bates Architects Sergison Bates Architects Sergison Bates Architects Sergison Bates Architects Sergison Bates Architects Sergison Bates Architects Sergison Bate

Burgoyne Middle School

Below
Burgoyne's new classroom is grafted onto the existing school building. Like the other two new buildings, it features large aluminium-clad rooflight lanterns, horizontal strip windows, spacious interiors, a strong use of colour that unifies and defines the structure, and a sheltered exterior deck.

Bottom
The faceted form also makes connections to each site through views and alignment to existing buildings and landscape.

Right
The principal interior space is a hall or studio with supporting spaces placed around it. Daylight enters from both the roof lantern and from a variety of windows or larger glazed doors.

Bates Architects Sergison Bates Architects Sergison Bates Architects Sergison Bates Architects Sergison Bates Architects Sergison Bates Architects Sergison Bates Architects Sergison Bates Architects Sergison Bates Architects Sergison Bate
Bates Architects Sergison Bates Architects Sergison Bates Architects Sergison Bates Architects Sergison Bates Architects Sergison Bates Architects Sergison Bates Architects Sergison Bates Architects Sergison Bates Architects Sergison Bate
Bates Architects Sergison Bates Architects Sergison Bates Architects Sergison Bates Architects Sergison Bates Architects Sergison Bates Architects Sergison Bates Architects Sergison Bates Architects Sergison Bates Architects Sergison Bate

Sandy Upper School

Left
The use of colour is fundamental in
the differentiation of each school.
The purpose-made windows have
coloured surrounds, and are treated
as long and low strips of glass in the
smaller spaces or as large picture
windows in the main spaces.

Below
The classroom building is the only
one of the three to be fully detached
from the existing school. It has an
inflected corner and a horizontal
hardwood boarding that clads it like
a screen wrapping around the
complex plan forms, in common
with the other two school buildings.

Passage, as well as the equally favoured sociorealist work of
the photographer Tony Ray-Jones. Each, in their own way,
encourages new ways of seeing the commonplace.

When Sergison and Bates talk of considering the discreet
qualities found in occupation and habitation – those things that
are 'ephemeral, in constant flux, individual and human', they
do not mean fleshing out their design with symbolic
ornamentation in homage to these qualities. Instead, they
engage in association, mediating idea and place by giving
attention to the ordinary, even mundane, elements of built
form that are 'touched, handled and brushed against' every
day, for instance internal linings and wearings, architraves,
skirtings and shutters. All of these are regarded as
opportunities to give spatial presence. So one side of an
architrave is widened to accommodate a light switch, and a
skirting board is extended upwards to make a dado lining; in
each case their customary consistency is disrupted in favour of
a specific expression and facilitation of use.

The influence of the Smithsons and their resounding
message of a new reinterpretation of orthodox
Modernism was an early call to order for the practice,
initially derived from their copious writings. As
intellectually motivated architects able to combine
writing and building, the two were consummate role
models. They are inspired by the work of Alvaro Siza,
the Portuguese architect, identifying with his sense of
context which aims to reveal rather than transform
meaning. There is a kinship between their attitude to
construction and his formal approach to buildings such
as his museum in Santiago, or the Evera low-cost
housing in Portugal for SAAL, the national housing
association, in which all nonessentials are removed.

Asked to consult as architects on the future
contextual framework of a large urban project such as
the Sittingbourne Settlements, together with East, back
in 1997, Sergison Bates's conceptual approach is able to

Bates Architects   Sergison Bates Architects   Sergison Bates Architects   Sergison Bates Architects   Sergison Bates Architects   Sergison Bates Architects   Sergison Bates Architects   Sergison Bates Architects   Sergison Bates Architects   Sergison Bates Architects   Sergison Bate
Bates Architects   Sergison Bates Architects   Sergison Bates Architects   Sergison Bates Architects   Sergison Bates Architects   Sergison Bates Architects   Sergison Bates Architects   Sergison Bates Architects   Sergison Bates Architects   Sergison Bates Architects   Sergison Bate
Bates Architects   Sergison Bates Architects   Sergison Bates Architects   Sergison Bates Architects   Sergison Bates Architects   Sergison Bates Architects   Sergison Bates Architects   Sergison Bates Architects   Sergison Bates Architects   Sergison Bates Architects   Sergison Bate

Sergison Bates Architects, Assisted self-build housing at Tilbury, Essex (2002)
Located on the Broadway Estate, a run-down and troubled 1960s housing estate, this is the first stage of a regeneration programme for the area. The timber veranda at first-floor level and raised boardwalk at ground level reflect the building's multiple occupancy and display the social spaces to the view of others. On the veranda side, walls are clad with a rain screen of larch-faced timber boards which extend to form the soffit of the overhanging canopy. The configuration of grain and knots, the flatness of the surface and the total enclosure of wood provide the benign associations of a protected environment.

extend to a larger scale of complexity. As a result of reading the grain of the landscape and the way it had become enclosed, the architects introduced an enabling structure – a new loose matrix of organising strips that offered a topographic arrangement to enable development to take place – into what were earth bunds, half a storey high, that delineated, protected and serviced land through drainage. The bunds became soft integrators, 'fingers of green' easing the natural demands of the site. Rather than proposing a uniform typology for siting the 550 houses required with an evenness of density, they enabled future development of an edge town that stood a chance of balancing a more internalised domesticity and an easy access to nature.

At Sittingbourne the architects were proposing to extend the limits of an existing and well-established suburban condition. They have written of their interest more generally in breaking with 'the myth of the vernacular'. Their output on housing to date represents a number of attempts, it seems, to posit specific design alternatives as 'closer representations of the vernacular than the current reliance on replicating the appearance of the past'. Moreover, their agenda extends to the advocacy of 'shattering the image of suburbia, to make way for the real demands of sustainability, cultural engagement and social opportunity'.

There is a quiet subversion, but most noticeably a consistency, running through all of the architects' projects. A sensibility to use a minimum number of materials and a reductive language is prevalent, which as a result requires a lot of coordination. Timber as a basis of structure is widespread. For example, the same claddings, Triboard and Pyroc, feature at both Wandsworth and Tilbury, public- and private-sector schemes. Detail throughout is suppressed into defined moments, not unlike Peter Zumthor's design for the Baths at Vals, where underneath the surface much is going on to achieve simplicity.

Sergison Bates's schemes also work with the idea of the horizontal section and a looseness of plan. As designs, they are closely adjusted to what was quite a complex site, for instance at Wandsworth the housing aligns itself to the geometries of the buildings. For three new classroom buildings commissioned by Bedfordshire County Council as part of the £13 million Department for Education and Skills 'Classrooms of the Future' scheme – Maple Tree Lower, Burgoyne Middle and Sandy Upper (infant, junior and secondary schools respectively) the architects were faced with a very complex site in terms of orientation, so the plan was arranged in order to achieve an asymmetrical form. The scheme afforded Sergison Bates considerable freedom in spatial organisation. At the outset the brief was not

Sergison Bates Architects Sergison Bates Architects Sergison Bates Architects Sergison Bates Architects Sergison Bates Architects Sergison Bates Architects Sergison Bates Architects Sergison Bates Architects Sergison Bates Architects Sergison Bat
n Bates Architects Sergison Bates Architects Sergison Bates Architects Sergison Bates Architects Sergison Bates Architects Sergison Bates Architects Sergison Bates Architects Sergison Bates Architects Sergison Bates Architects Sergison Bates Architects Sergison Bat
n Bates Architects Sergison Bates Architects Sergison Bates Architects Sergison Bates Architects Sergison Bates Architects Sergison Bates Architects Sergison Bates Architects Sergison Bates Architects Sergison Bates Architects Sergison Bat
n Bates Architects Sergison Bates Architects Sergison Bates Architects Sergison Bates Architects Sergison Bates Architects Sergison Bates Architects Sergison Bates Architects Sergison Bates Architects Sergison Bat

Left
Sergison Bates Architects, Housing, studios and offices, Wandsworth, London, 2003
Converting and extending the old Wandsworth Workshops paint-factory building dating from the 1930s into a six-storey apartment building, the architects have added a timber-framed single-storey extension on top of the roof to house 11 apartments. Supported on a steel transfer structure, it absorbs the gently faceted form of the existing building to create a continuous mat-like surface. Entry to the apartments is via a timber-decked covered walkway (inset) and, in front of the individual entrances, open-air courtyards.

Right
Sergison Bates Architects, Prototype semi-detached housing, Stevenage, Hertfordshire, 2000
The practice was invited by the William Sutton Trust to develop innovative ideas for semi-detached housing. The street frontage shows the splayed facade and double-pitched roof, describing the dual occupancy that traditional, single-roofed semi-detached houses do not. The angled planes create two distinct faces: an intimate street frontage (inset) and a more private rear. The timber-panel structure is prefabricated and load bearing, with industrially produced 'slate' tiles and brick slips assembled in panels, both in earth-based cladding colours, relating to the rural character of the location.

fully formulated, and the practice worked closely with the head teachers on its evolution. Encouraged by them to make a circular classroom, the three spaces each ended up as hexagons. The architects tried to strike a balance between the fact that this was a pilot project for a replicable prototype and the need for each building to be specific by developing a number of elements that were repeatable. In plan, each of the three school buildings consists of a central, top-lit room with ancillary spaces and a covered entrance, timber-framed walls, a timber rain-screen cladding feature, with a mix of horizontal windows and floor-to-ceiling sliding doors with brightly coloured frames.

Earlier work by the practice shows that the architects prefer individual rather than replicated solutions. With their three 'Classrooms of the Future', for which repeatable solutions that are also sustainable were desirable, they have created a formal language of architecture and typology that is adaptable and identifiable rather than standardised. Pushing their personal brief for authenticity and a legibility in construction, the floor decking is also used as a rain screen; soffits are partly unpainted and this, together with the treatment of junctions, means that the construction is visible.

The three schools reflect the architects' interest in conceptualising construction through their treatment of cladding as a wrapping. This is not necessarily either a rational or a consistent approach but one influenced by a spatial concern. Allied to this, they use colour in a painterly way to create individually identifiable spaces.

The scheme for assisted self-build housing at Tilbury in Essex (2001–02), within the Thames Gateway area, is just as direct in what it is doing. It sits off the ground on feet; nothing is there that is not doing a job, piecing together the site, yet it achieves a strong overall presence. Located in the run-down and troubled 1960s Broadway housing estate, it was the initial part of a regeneration programme for the area. Replacing an area of disused open ground at the edge of the site, it consists of an apartment building with a landscaped courtyard. The intention was to develop affordable housing through a building and apartment typology that would appeal to young people and not replicate the predominant terrace typology. To the east the facade has a formal frontage; to the west a more informal appearance, as the building with its timber veranda and

Bates Architects Sergison Bates Architects Sergison Bates Architects Sergison Bates Architects Sergison Bates Architects Sergison Bates Architects Sergison Bates Architects Sergison Bates Architects Sergison Bates Architects Sergison Bates Architects Sergison Bates
Bates Architects Sergison Bates Architects Sergison Bates Architects Sergison Bates Architects Sergison Bates Architects Sergison Bates Architects Sergison Bates Architects Sergison Bates Architects Sergison Bates Architects Sergison Bates Architects Sergison Bates
Bates Architects Sergison Bates Architects Sergison Bates Architects Sergison Bates Architects Sergison Bates Architects Sergison Bates Architects Sergison Bates Architects Sergison Bates Architects Sergison Bates Architects Sergison Bates Architects Sergison Bates

Below
Sergison Bates with Caruso St John, public house, Walsall, West Midlands, 1998
Walsall's Wharf development, including Caruso St John's Art Gallery, made provision for a square and a pub adjacent to the canal basin. Sergison Bates pursued the design in line with Caruso St John's view that it should be a neighbour to the gallery. The dark, almost sombre

building with its concrete-tiled roof and aluminium guttering has simple yet appropriate elevations (west shown here) on the canal side, long and glazed, with a separation between cladding and structure, and inside a simple L-shaped bar and drinking area. A line of timber posts and beams punctuates the space.

overhanging roof is placed within a courtyard. The architects liken the housing to the condominiums often found in social housing on the west coast of the US. Choosing self-build, with locals – not a common way to realise housing – gave them an impetus to source original facing materials designed to exploit and highlight the simplicity of frame construction.

Sergison Bates's scheme for housing, studios and offices in Wandsworth (2003) is a refurbishment, extension and densification of an existing paint-factory building – Wandsworth Workshops – built in the 1930s alongside the bedraggled beds of the River Wandle, opposite a supermarket and close to the town centre. The architects have added a timber-framed single-storey extension on top of the existing roof. Supported on a steel transfer structure, the new building includes 11 apartments, some live/work units, a medical centre and a café, and creates a continuous mat-like structure on the gently faceted form of the existing structure. The apartments are reached via timber-decked covered walkways with a consistent grain of pine; each has individual open-air courtyards; pre-galvanised aluminium sheeting on the openings, canopies and letter boxes; and Douglas fir doors and window frames. The hermetic nature of the dwellings is played off against the communal atmosphere of the walkways.

Everything is at 90 degrees, with no mitred elements – a simple room arrangement around a central hall with living rooms and bedrooms opening on to covered balconies. At the southern end of the site is a new apartment building. The concrete flat slab and column structure is faceted in plan as it follows the boundary of the site and continues the undulating form of the existing workshop buildings.

The architects' concern with what they call 'reduced form-making, based on the familiar images of buildings' is demonstrable in their design for a public house in Walsall, in

the West Midlands. Once again they use linings and claddings to lend the building expression through their layering, material, volume and, above all, associative power with familiar images. The external faces of the building are clad in facing materials of equal colour and texture which reinforces the volume of the whole rather than the detail of each part. The building's shed-like appearance gives it a similar feel to neighbouring warehouses and superstores. The inclusion of an outsized, enclosing roof, adjusted in line with the footprint of the site, creates a fairly unusual set of proportions that conveys its public identity without recourse to historical precedents.

The design for a prototype house built in Stevenage for the William Sutton Trust became a means by which Sergison Bates could speculate on the house-like image of the ubiquitous semi. Reinforcing the form by a minimum expression of joins and overlaps between materials and surfaces, the architects here make the roof and wall cladding continuous, and arrange the windows freely to allow walls and roof to appear part of a seamless flow. Rather in the manner of the strategy for the public house in Walsall, in which the whole volume instead of individual details is reinforced, this tactic applies a language of protection, a metaphorical stance that promotes the 'dwelling' experience of a house. ⚙

Lucy Bullivant is an architectural critic, author and curator. She has curated many exhibitions and symposia including 'The Near and the Far' (Milan Triennale, 1996), 'Spaced Out' (ICA, 1997), 'Kid Size' (Vitra Design Museum, 1997), 'Space Invaders: New UK Architecture' (British Council, 2001), Archis magazine's London events series (1998–01) and '4dspace' (ICA, 2003). She contributes to many international publications, including Domus and Archis, and guest-edited 'Home Front: New Developments in Housing', the July/August 2003 issue of Architectural Design. She is writing a new book on emerging UK architects for Thames & Hudson.

Resumé
Sergison Bates Architects

1996	Stephen Bates and Jonathan Sergison establish practice in London
	Montessori Nursery School, London W9
	Refurbishment and new-build for Windmill Montessori School, in collaboration with Bennetts Associates

1998	Studio building refurbishment, London EC1, for Cartlidge Levene Design
	Sotheby's Refurbishment, London W1; exhibition and display galleries in collaboration with Bennetts Associates
	Public house, Walsall; winner of 1999 CAMRA Best Pub Award; new-build pub for Chartwell Land, in collaboration with Caruso St John

1999	Office building refurbishment, London W1, for Derwent Valley Holdings plc, in collaboration with Bennetts Associates
	Social housing development, London N1; special-needs housing for New Islington & Hackney Housing Association
	Prototype garden office building, Soho, for Corus (British Steel), in collaboration with FM Design
	Urban improvement works for the London Borough of Southwark

1999–2000	Graz-Maribor land-use study, Austria/Slovenia; regional strategic study for the Zentralvereinigung der Architekten – Steiermark
	Social housing prototype, Stevenage, for William Sutton Trust; Housing Design Awards Special Commendation

2000	Flexible school buildings pilot project; modular classroom buildings for Essex County Council (competition short list)
	Studio building addition, London W10; loft office/studios for Clobb Properties

2001	Urban housing, King's Cross, London
	Apartment building for Rooff Ltd

Development; medical centre, Wandsworth, London

2002	Office building, Clerkenwell, London
	Urban design framework study, Barking; strategic urban development study for the London Borough of Barking and Dagenham, in collaboration with East
	Assisted self-build housing for New Essex Housing Association; housing development, Tilbury, Essex; Housing Design Project Award 2003
	Office Building, Vauxhall, London

2003	Urban design framework study, Woolwich; strategic urban development study for the London Borough of Greenwich/LDA, in collaboration with East
	'Classrooms of the Future', Bedfordshire; three new classroom buildings for Bedfordshire County Council
	Wandsworth Workshops, London SW18; refurbishment of former paint factory for B1 use and new residential extension and apartment building for Baylight Properties
	Apartment building and school building refurbishment, Woolwich; refurbishment of two existing school buildings (one grade 2 listed) and construction of new apartment building to form new residential development for Tilfen Land
	Woolwich Arsenal master plan, Woolwich; master-plan study for 3,000 new dwellings, leisure and commercial space for Berkley Homes (East Thames) Ltd

After the Festival
Before Rock'n'Roll

Half a century after Kadleigh, Whitfield and
Horsburgh first revealed their plans for
London's Barbican site in the City, the first
major book on the design of the Barbican
is to be published by Wiley-Academy.
Its author, **David Heathcote**, explains
how amidst the doldrums and greyness
of postwar London, Chamberlin, Powell
and Bon landed the commission.

Fifty years ago London must have seemed an anticlimactic sort of a place. The evening dances to calypsos on the South Bank during the Festival of Britain were long passed, Everest had been conquered and the new queen crowned. Yet the centre of the Commonwealth lay as blackened and derelict as it had been after the Blitz a decade before. Rationing, a housing crisis and traffic jams were a constant reminder of what had yet to be done. Despite the efforts of two postwar governments of different hues, nothing seemed to change. In the City only a dozen or so acres of bomb site had benefited from reconstruction.

The situation was sufficiently bad for the Lord Mayor of London to complain to Parliament that building controls were strangling the City's efforts to rebuild. Into the breach stepped, of course, a committee, though one led by a hero of committees, the recently knighted Sir Gerald Barry, former director-general and chairman of the Festival of Britain. This group set its sights on redeveloping the City's largest and oldest Blitz site – the Orwellian-named areas 2 and 4 north of route 11, then becoming known as the Barbican. The question was, 'What was it to be?' The planners, with their eye on immortality, had spent a lot of time reinventing St Paul's and other more glamorous parts of the City, but the idea for the Barbican was to return it to its former status

as an area of commerce. The Corporation of London had previously had high hopes for a trade centre for the textile industry. However, this proposal had fallen through in 1951 and the corporation had fallen back on the idea of rampant office development; Charles Clore was thinking of developing 5 acres of the 40-acre site – surely others would follow.

But Barry's New Barbican Committee had bigger ideas, and in the spirit of the moment set its sights on wholesale comprehensive development – a massive scheme that would fill the entire site. Its architects were the young partnership of Kadleigh, Whitfield and Horsburgh, chosen because of Kadleigh's and Horsburgh's radical proposals for redeveloping Paddington, published late in 1952.

High Paddington was a scheme to house 8,000 residents of the borough in a tight complex of point blocks joined by equally high terraces, overlooking a massive podium, 600 feet across, pierced by lunettes providing light for the marshalling yard it was proposed the development would cover. This would allow much of the surrounding housing to be demolished and turned into parkland. Each of the dwellings in the 300-foot blocks was to enjoy

BARBICAN PENTHOUSE OVER THE CITY
DAVID HEATHCOTE

a double-height garden/balcony, and it was proposed that
this Corbusian motif be extended to include two primary
schools, a hotel, hospital and a church on the top of the
blocks. A more discreet attraction of the scheme was that
the construction could be carried out using the railway
system below without choking the surrounding road system
with construction traffic. Leaving aside the debt to Le
Corbusier, Kadleigh's experience in the logistical work
behind the Berlin Luftbrucke and Horsburgh's studies
of Italian hill towns provided the basis for this radical
intervention into the self-consciously comfy world of
housing reconstruction of the day.

The New Barbican Committee clearly saw the potential
of the ideas behind High Paddington for the Barbican site,
which was traversed by a railway line with access to the
national network, and also had a small marshalling yard.

In late July 1954, the architects presented their proposal for
New Barbican – a design on an even more heroic scale than
High Paddington. The development took full advantage of the
vertical potential of the site by proposing that it be excavated
to 60 feet below ground level and rise to 300 feet above it.
Housing for around 7,000 people as well as offices,
warehouses, a trade centre, community facilities, gardens, car
parks, and road and rail distribution routes could be fitted into
this space, meaning the development would need
to be considered for New Town planning permission.

The existing railway would be left on an embankment 30
feet below street level and 30 feet above. Rail lines would
lead from this embankment down to sidings serving
warehouses that would rise four storeys to ground level.
These would also be served by a road system up to ground
level through two spiral road ramps. Sitting on top of this
underground complex were to be a further three storeys of
factory or commercial development, including five-storey

office blocks. These in turn would surround a 7-acre
park and themselves form a podium for the rest of the
development and 10 acres of podium gardens. On the
podium, as well as access roads, there would be four
storeys of maisonettes arranged in continuous
hexaform ribbons, and above these five point blocks of
varying sizes and heights made up of offices in the
lower storeys with flats above.

The fantastic Perspex model of the project, which
was determinedly vague about details, was exhibited
at the Houses of Parliament but through this the
project gained nothing more than notoriety and good
reviews in the professional press. Both the
Corporation and the London County Council quietly set
their faces against the project, which in the end was
rejected by Duncan Sandys, Minister for Housing and
Local Government. However, the project did stir these
authorities to develop their own comprehensive plans
for the Barbican. Indeed, the Corporation produced
two plans (as a result of internal divisions) one of
which, by architects Chamberlin, Powell and Bon,
was particularly favoured by the minister, leading him
to recommend in a letter to the Corporation that the
Barbican be redeveloped as:

a genuine residential neighbourhood incorporating
schools, shops, open spaces and other amenities,
even if this means foregoing a more remunerative
return on the land.

That was in 1956. However, it was a generation
later, when Kadleigh, Chamberlin and Elvis were
long dead, that the Queen at last opened one of
the great monuments to the spirit of reconstruction
– Chamberlin, Powell and Bon's Barbican. ᗐ

'LACKING THE LACK': The Museum of the History of the Hellenic World, Athens

Nikos Georgiadis, a principal of Anamorphosis Architects, the practice designing the new Museum of the History of the Hellenic World in Athens (scheduled on site in 2006), describes how the architects developed a strategy that turned history to their advantage. Embracing 'the lack' of significant surviving Hellenic pieces, Anamorphosis resolved to reactivate the physicality of historic forms and design a spatial monument.

Anamorphosis Architects, Museum of the Hellenic World, Athens (due on site 2006)

Below
View from the south.

Opposite
Northeastern view of the amphitheatre, dome and (self-)sheltering cell.

Designing a museum of history, not original historical pieces, from the outset introduces the question of how to present the actual mode of the untimely as a material of permanent interest beyond any historicist contemplation and consciousness. To exhibit not just objects of identity (national or other) but also the way in which history documents itself is a museological paradox/challenge as well as an exceptional psychoanalytic process; yet such a challenge/project becomes more compelling due to the fact that many significant pieces concerning Hellenism are missing (destroyed, removed, 'saved' elsewhere ...). This already contextualises design in critical opposition to today's 'museum culture' and the dominant notions of 'collection' and 'acquisition' – emblematic of the ideology of the all-seeing (-possessing) curious and simultaneously disinterested postmodern spectator/ego.[1]

Anamorphosis Architects distinguishes between the historical and the historic, that is, the way we see (objectify) history through symbolic ideals, prejudices and nostalgia, and the way history sees us, by returning as an a-chronic event engaging us in unsymbolic procedures. If in standard psychoanalytic terms history is conceived as an unexpected comeback in the field of the 'symptom', in the method of anamorphosis history is conceived – beyond the mere symptomatic disruption – as an extended spatial modality capable of generating principles for design.[2] Moreover, in the case of Greek history, this approach recognises a profound psychoanalytic structure in the permanent exchange, across the Aegean Sea, between Greece and Asia Minor – the motherland and the 'opposite side': a side both *own* and *unknown*.

The 'missing' of the authentic pieces is seen as guidance rather than disadvantage. The psychoanalytic concept of 'lack' (J Lacan) becomes the main design principle. Lack is the spatial critique of the narcissistic making (or unmaking) of the object; it involves both a familiarisation with the loss of it (the original piece, the beloved) and a creative spatial process

of overcoming loss after the completion of mourning. As opposed to absence, lack indicates the persistence of the morphic principle beyond the symbolic ties. It activates the dialectic of positive appearance and 'accomplishedness' – concepts that are neutralised/foreclosed by narcissism. It shifts the question from the eternal quest of identity, pleasure and the object, to the discourse of fulfilment itself and its spatial assertiveness. Yet in this context lack has been deeply and repeatedly experienced in Greek history, becoming an exceptionally real, as opposed to textual, condition inspiring rich spatial propositions.[3]

Spatiality in the context of lack is both the major diachronic documentation of Greek civilisation and a critical design concept. Space, instead of becoming a neutral canvas/source for an eclectic commemoration (objectification) of the past or for an application of negativity and endless melancholic lamenting over the lost property,[4] is hereby activated through recurring, homeomorphing and collocating[5] processes: a simultaneous dialectic of building and exhibits. Anamorphosis designs a spatial monument[1] by reactivating the physicality of historic forms. The 'amphitheatre', the 'dome' and the '(self-)sheltering structure' share a natural homeomorphy capable of binding a spatial scenario.

These are neither symbolic nor abstract sculptural themes but real spatial experiences (involving distinct qualities of lighting, material and collective function) constantly appearing in various instances and roles throughout Greek history and thus manifesting an intelligence of their own. They are resynthesised in one continuous self-anamorphosed surface: a gesture of morphic persistence and exchangeability across the building, which produces the three major spatial

Anamorphosis Architects, Museum of the History of the Hellenic World, Athens –
performance of light, material and function.

Top
The dome – Byzantium installation.

Bottom left
The amphitheatre - Classical Antiquity installation.

Bottom right
The (self-)sheltering cell screens – Modern Times installation.

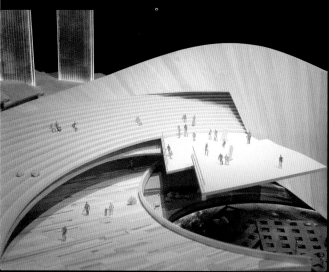

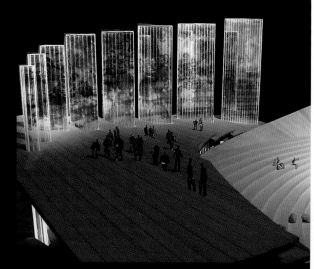

Top
The morphic documentation of the Hellenic world.

Bottom
The self-anamorphosed surface. Recurring, homeomorphing, collocating.

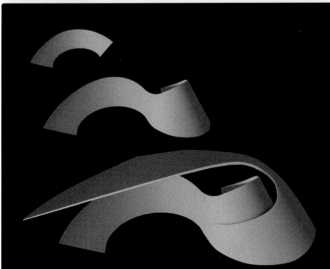

installations of the museum: the amphitheatre presenting Classical Antiquity, the dome presenting Byzantium, and the (self-)sheltering cell (covering the overall museum space) presenting Modern Times: 17th to early 20th century (the ultimate expatriation of the Greeks from Asia Minor).

The three installations are distinct spatial experiences elaborated at the levels of lighting and collective function, including respectively bright daylight, small sharp shadows and meeting; indirect ambient light, no shadows and congregation; moving image, cinematic sidelighting, long shadows and audience/crowd gathering. Yet the strip surface employs a gradient synthesis of materials and construction techniques varying from tectonic, marble, stone, cast material, spolio, timber, glass and metal structures.

The design of the Museum of the History of the Hellenic World[6] proposes a spatial museology by conceiving the museum, in principle, as a building of lack rather than object-display. Mainstream scenariocentric museology is based precisely on the appropriation/ foreclosure of the concept of lack, by neutralising it as object-'scarcity', -'preciousness', -'uniqueness'. However, lack is the spatial dialectic that reveals the principle of presentation/design as a mode embedded in the very realness of the exhibited, and in turn reactivates it as a new transferential process and condition of interest. ⚙

Notes

1 This contextualisation was introduced by Anamorphosis Architects, overtaking an earlier scenariocentric museological approach. A critique of the postmodern museum culture and indifferent subjectivity (D Sherman, I Rogoff) appears in N Georgiadis, 'The museum as spatial ritual in the completion of mourning', A+T, no 2, 2004. The article criticises the museological notions of 'museum without walls', 'en filade', 'white cube' and scenariocentric 'new correspondences' (see R Greenberg, B Ferguson and S Nairne (eds), Thinking About Exhibitions, Routledge (London), 1996, and Douglas Crimp, On the Museum's Ruins, MIT Press (Cambridge, MA), 1993).
2 This method is based on N Georgiadis's theory of anamorphosis: a spatial approach of Lacanian psychoanalysis, and critique of the theories of 'deconstruction', 'fold' and 'universal pragmatics'. It has been presented by the author at conferences, in university lectures, publications and interviews.
3 A remarkable example appears in Thucydides's 'Epitaph', in which the obituary for the dead is carried through a simultaneous praise of the city/space of Athens. It is also common in Greek tradition that monuments are built on – and with – the ruins of pre-existing monuments.
4 By using the concept of 'lack', Anamorphosis Architects has elaborated three projects proposing a spatial critique against applied negativity and negated space. These are: the New Acropolis Museum, competition entry, 1990 (see 'Tracing Architecture', Architectural Design, vol 68, 3–4, 1998); the Remodelling of the Marathon's Starting Site, Marathon, competition entry, 1992; the Museum of the History of the Hellenic World, completion due 2006.
5 Concepts presented by the author at 'Positions in Architecture' international conference, ICA London, November 2000.
6 The project was exhibited at the 8th Venice Architectural Biennale – 'Next 2002', presented at 'Positions in Architecture', ICA, London, November 2000, and published in Vivian Constantinopoulos, 10x10, Phaidon Press (London), 2000, pp 41–3 See also www.anamorphosis-architects.com.

Nikos Georgiadis, a founding member of Anamorphosis Architects, is also an internationally published architectural writer and theorist, and teaches at the Architectural Department, University of Patras, Greece. He was the editor of the 1998 'Tracing Architecture' title of Architectural Design.

Anamorphosis Architects: Nikos Georgiadis, Tota Mamalaki, Kostas Kakoyiannis, Vaios Zitonoulis.

ÉCOLE POLYTECHNIQUE FÉDÉRALE DE LAUSANNE

Learning Center
at the Swiss Federal Institute of Technology in Lausanne

The Swiss Federal Institute of Technology in Lausanne plans to build what will become the new heart of its campus: an extensive library to cater to the needs of some 9,500 students, researchers and staff.

This new building will be the place where one comes, alone or as a group, to build further knowledge, share information, exchange ideas and envision new solutions. This will be a learning center for a new generation, where all information is available to the whole community, be it network-based or through traditional media.

But also a place to live in, with its restaurants, exhibition halls and conference rooms. A forum in the heart of a campus undergoing a deep mutation.

A symbolic place which shall reflect EPFL identity, dynamism and development, as well as its innovative capacity and involvement in numerous challenges with global reach.

In order to give shape to this project, the EPFL launches an international architectural competition;

interested architects should submit prequalification documents in order to enter the restricted procedure for the commissioned parallel study of its preliminary architectural design. Further information on the prequalification procedure may be obtained :

EPFL
DII / Service des constructions et d'exploitation
BS - Ecublens
CH-1015 Lausanne
Switzerland

or on the web site : http://learningcenter.epfl.ch/

Application files shall reach the Project Owner latest on **April 16th 2004 at 12 noon**.

Book Review

Asmara: Africas Secret Modernist City
Edward Deinson, Guang Yu Ren and Naigzy Gebremedhin

ISBN 1 85894 209 8 Hardback £35.00 240 pages
Published by Merrell, London, October 2003

Following the declaration of Eritrea's independence from Ethiopia in 1991, the city of Asmara has been 'discovered' and there has been a growing awareness of its architectural significance. Built almost entirely in the 1930s by Italians, it has one of the highest concentrations of Modernist architecture anywhere in the world. Desperate to build quickly, the colonial government of the time allowed radical architectural experimentation and thus the city became the ultimate in Modern Movement urbanism. Asmara's extraordinary history and geographical location have meant that this architectural legacy escaped wartime destruction and survives today for all to see.

The book tells the story of the city and its architectural development. The introduction covers, in ten chapters, the history of the city from its beginnings in 1889 through its incredible development under Italian Fascist rule to its independence and present-day position, and goes on to postulate what the future may hold. With details of both the architectural and political development it provides a comprehensive explanation of Eritrean roots and the development of Asmara itself.

General Baldissera first arrived on the plain that was to become Asmara in 1889, marking the beginning of Italy's presence in the area. Then, as a mark of their power in the area, the Italians developed Asmara into the capital of the colony. This historical development is illustrated in astonishing detail with contemporary drawings, maps and photographs from each period. Naturally some of the details are quite harrowing – as this was a city being built under a fascist regime. As a result, the native Eritrean area of the city was kept in poverty, whilst the Italians lived in comfort and luxury. This is reflected today as the area has remained one of the most neglected suburbs, though work is now afoot to redress the balance.

Following this powerful essay the reader is taken on a lavish visual tour – in chronological order – of the individual buildings that make up the city, during which the echos of Adolf Loos, Alvar Aalto, Le Corbusier, Louis Kahn, Eric Mendelsohn and other greats leap out from the page. As one would expect, some of the imitations don't quite reach the genius of the masters, but for the most part the buildings show talent and daring – huge concrete cantilevers, beautiful smooth curves, majestic halls and clever facades.

A number of the buildings are now in a desperate state of repair, and much work needs to be done to save the city. However, the work of the Cultural Assets Rehabilitation Project, of which one of the authors of the book is a director, is set to ensure its conservation.

That all these inspirational examples of such a period of architectural innovation survive in one city is incredible; that there is such a comprehensive and well-organised book to celebrate such a feat is gratifying.
Reviewed by Maggie Toy

∆D Book Club
Architectural Design

Get inspired – with these fantastic offers on a range of Wiley-Academy's innovative design titles

Confessions: Principles Architecture Process Life
Jan Kaplicky
Confessions offers an insight into the mind of Future Systems architect Jan Kaplicky – his ideas, opinions and sources of inspiration. With an equal balance of images and textual observations, it is both visually and mentally engaging, and is an incredibly personal and honest account.

0-471-49541-7; 204pp; August 2002;
Paperback; ~~£24.95~~ £14.97

The Four States of Architecture
Hanrahan + Meyers Architects
The first book to chart the talent of exceptional New York firm, Hanrahan + Meyers, with support, via written contributions, from key figures such as Robert Stern and Bernard Tschumi

0-471-49652-9; 128pp; April 2002;
Paperback; ~~£24.95~~ £14.97

Sustaining Architecture in the Anti-Machine Age
Ian Abley
This book brings together contributions from a range of architects, journalists, academics and consultants, approaching sustainability from a wide variety of viewpoints. Each chapter includes a robust, lively text, illustrated with carefully chosen exemplar projects.

0-471-48660-4; 240pp January 2002;
Paperback; ~~£19.99~~ £11.99

First House
Christian Bjone
Covers the first works of a group of key architects who were teaching and/or studying at Harvard between the late 1930s and the early 1950s. Includes first houses by Gropius and Breuer, Ulrich Franzen, Philip Johnson, Paul Rudolph and IM Pei
"...beautifully produced clever and thoughtful..."
—**The Twentieth-Century Society Newsletter**

0-470-84538-4; 224pp; April 2002;
Hardback; ~~£39.95~~ £23.97

Archi-toons: Funniness, Comedy and Delight
Richard T Bynum
Explore the lighter side of architecture with this volume of humorous cartoons from the internationally renowned architect and popular cartoonist and illustrator Rick Bynum. These cartoons take a quirky, witty, insightful and sometimes irreverent look at the world of design, architecture and construction.

0-470-85406-5; 128pp; April 2003; Paperback;
~~£9.99~~ £6.00

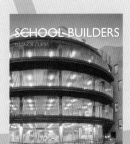

School Builders
Eleanor Curtis
School Builders provides a fascinating overview of the latest developments in school design from around the world. Packed with construction methods, case studies, outstanding imagery and technical plans, it offers an indispensable guide for planning and designing school buildings, from primary through to high schools.

0-471-62377-6; 224pp; January 2003;
Hardback; ~~£50.00~~ £30.00

Encyclopaedia of Architectural Technology
Jacqueline Glass
A comprehensive guide to architectural technology, that encompasses every aspect of modern construction. Including several hundred entries in alphabetical order with diagrams and illustrations, this is an essential guide for the architect and student alike
"More than a mere dictionary of architectural terms...a useful reference tome with a detailed explanation of many key terms."
—**Architects Journal**

0-471-88559-2; 360pp; February 2002;
Hardback; ~~£60.00~~ £36.00

Subscribe Now

As an influential and prestigious architectural publication, *Architectural Design* has an almost unrivalled reputation worldwide. Published bimonthly, it successfully combines the currency and topicality of a newsstand journal with the editorial rigour and design qualities of a book. Consistently at the forefront of cultural thought and design since the 1960s, it has time and again proved provocative and inspirational – inspiring theoretical, creative and technological advances. Prominent in the 1980s for the part it played in Postmodernism and then in Deconstruction, *D* has recently taken a pioneering role in the technological revolution of the 1990s. With groundbreaking titles dealing with cyberspace and hypersurface architecture, it has pursued the conceptual and critical implications of high-end computer software and virtual realities. *D*

D Architectural Design

SUBSCRIPTION RATES 2004
Institutional Rate: UK £160
Personal Rate: UK £99
Discount Student* Rate: UK £70
OUTSIDE UK
Institutional Rate: US $240
Personal Rate: US $150
Student* Rate: US $105

*Proof of studentship will be required when placing an order. Prices reflect rates for a 2002 subscription and are subject to change without notice.

TO SUBSCRIBE
Phone your credit card order:
+44 (0)1243 843 828

Fax your credit card order to:
+44 (0)1243 770 432

Email your credit card order to:
cs-journals@wiley.co.uk

Post your credit card or cheque order to:
John Wiley & Sons Ltd.
Journals Administration Department
1 Oldlands Way
Bognor Regis
West Sussex PO22 9SA
UK

Please include your postal delivery address with your

All *D* volumes are availab
To place an order please w
John Wiley & Sons Ltd
Customer Services
1 Oldlands Way
Bognor Regis
West Sussex PO22 9SA

Please quote the ISBN number of the iss you are ordering.

D is available to purchase on both a subscription basis and as individual vol

---

○ I wish to subscribe to *D* *Architectural Design* at the **Institutional rate of £160**.

○ I wish to subscribe to *D* *Architectural Design* at the **Personal rate of £99**.

○ I wish to subscribe to *D* *Architectural Design* at the **Student rate of £70**.

○ *D* *Architectural Design* is available to individuals on either a calendar year or rolling annual basis; Institutional subscriptions are only available on a calendar year basis. Tick this box if you would like your Personal or Student subscription on a rolling annual basis.

○ Payment enclosed by Cheque/Money order/Drafts.

Value/Currency £/US$ [   ]

○ Please charge £/US$ [   ] to my credit card.
Account number:

[ ][ ][ ][ ][ ][ ][ ][ ][ ][ ][ ][ ][ ][ ][ ][ ][ ]

Expiry date:

[ ][ ][ ][ ][ ][ ]

Card: Visa/Amex/Mastercard/Eurocard *(delete as applicable)*

Cardholder's signature [   ]

Cardholder's name [   ]

Address [   ]

[   ]

[   ] Post/Zip Code [   ]

Recipient's name [   ]

Address [   ]

[   ]

[   ] Post/Zip Code [   ]

I would like to buy the following issues at £22.50 each:

○ *D* 168 *Extreme Sites*, Deborah Gans + Claire Weisz

○ *D* 167 *Property Development*, David Sokol

○ *D* 166 *Club Culture*, Eleanor Curtis

○ *D* 165 *Urban Flashes Asia*, Nicholas Boyarsky + Peter Lang

○ *D* 164 *Home Front: New Developments in Housing*, Lucy Bullivant

○ *D* 163 *Art + Architecture*, Ivan Margolius

○ *D* 162 *Surface Consciousness*, Mark Taylor

○ *D* 161 *Off the Radar*, Brian Carter + Annette LeCuyer

○ *D* 160 *Food + Architecture*, Karen A Franck

○ *D* 159 *Versioning in Architecture*, SHoP

○ *D* 158 *Furniture + Architecture*, Edwin Heathcote

○ *D* 157 *Reflexive Architecture*, Neil Spiller

○ *D* 156 *Poetics in Architecture*, Leon van Schaik

○ *D* 155 *Contemporary Techniques in Architecture*, Ali Rahim

○ *D* 154 *Fame and Architecture*, J. Chance and T. Schmiedeknecht

○ *D* 153 *Looking Back in Envy*, Jan Kaplicky

○ *D* 152 *Green Architecture*, Brian Edwards

○ *D* 151 *New Babylonians*, Iain Borden + Sandy McCreery

○ *D* 150 *Architecture + Animation*, Bob Fear

○ *D* 149 *Young Blood*, Neil Spiller

○ *D* 148 *Fashion and Architecture*, Martin Pawley

○ *D* 147 *The Tragic in Architecture*, Richard Patterson

○ *D* 146 *The Transformable House*, Jonathan Bell and Sally Godwin

○ *D* 145 *Contemporary Processes in Architecture*, Ali Rahim

○ *D* 144 *Space Architecture*, Dr Rachel Armstrong

○ *D* 143 *Architecture and Film II*, Bob Fear

○ *D* 142 *Millennium Architecture*, Maggie Toy and Charles Jencks

Oboe

The fun way to learn!

Sarah Watts

kevin
mayhew

kevin mayhew

First published in Great Britain in 2003 by Kevin Mayhew Ltd
Buxhall, Stowmarket, Suffolk IP14 3BW
Tel: +44 (0) 1449 737978 Fax: +44 (0) 1449 737834
E-mail: info@kevinmayhewltd.com

www.kevinmayhew.com

ISBN 978 1 84417 043 2
ISMN M 57024 180 4
Catalogue No. 3611737

Cover design: Rob Mortonson
Music setting: Donald Thomson
Proof reader: Tracy Cook

Printed and bound in Great Britain

Contents

A note from the composer

This is a fun book of jazzy pieces with a 'feel good' accompaniment to encourage you in the early stages of learning.

Although *Razzamajazz* is not a tutor, I hope you will enjoy learning the pieces and benefit from them.

SARAH WATTS

Introducing B

This is where it goes on the music

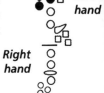

To play B
press the keys
coloured black

Left hand

Right hand

B GROOVY

NOTE USED - B

4

here's A

This is where it goes on the music

To play A
press the keys
coloured black

Left
hand

Right
hand

TWO AT
TWILIGHT

NOTES USED - B, A

5

now for G

This is where it goes on the music

To play G press the keys coloured black

Left hand

Right hand

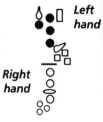

STARDOM WALTZ

NOTES USED - B, A, G

STRIPY CAT CRAWL

NOTES USED - B, A

... and now C

To play C press the keys coloured black

Left hand

Right hand

This is where it goes on the music

MR COOL

NOTES USED - B, A, G, C

Swing (♩ = 130)

(♫ = ♩♪)

Optional vocals (spoken):

Yeh!   U-huh!   Hit it!

That's cool!   Yeh!

U-huh!   Hit it!   I'm done!

9

KIM'S BALLAD

NOTES USED - B, A, G, C

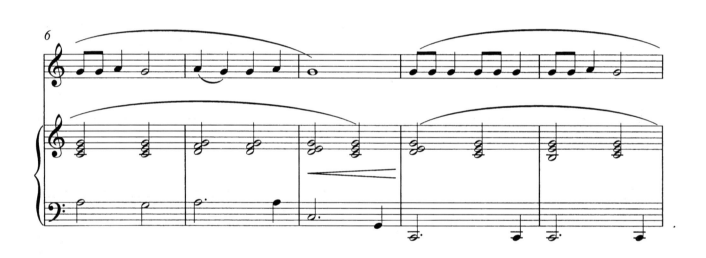

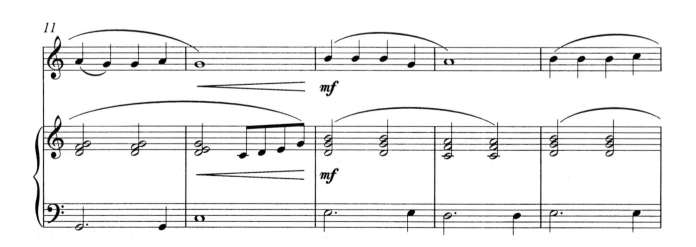

and next D

This is where it goes on the music

To play D press the keys coloured black

Left hand

Right hand

MOVIE BUSTER

NOTES USED - B, A, G, C, D

MELLOW OUT

NOTES USED - B, A, G, C, D

14

15

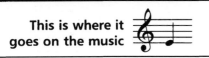

and on to E

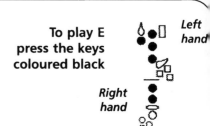

To play E
press the keys
coloured black

Left
hand

Right
hand

**This is where it
goes on the music**

WATER LILIES

NOTES USED - G, A, B, C, D, E

© Copyright 2003 Kevin Mayhew Ltd.
It is illegal to photocopy music.

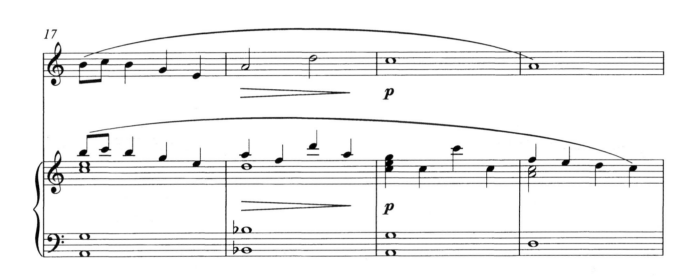

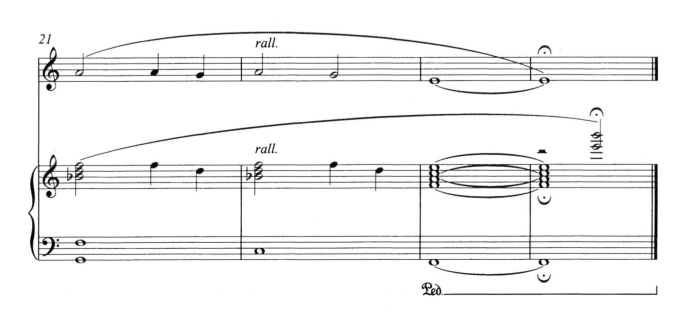

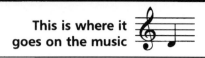

here's low D

This is where it goes on the music

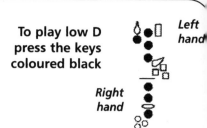

To play low D press the keys coloured black

Left hand

Right hand

TEN TOE TAPPER

NOTES USED - G, A, B, C, D, E, low D

13 *Tap dance! (or Woodblock solo)*

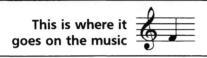

now for F

This is where it goes on the music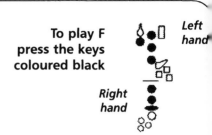

PLAY OF LIGHT

NOTES USED - G, A, B, C, D, E, low D, F

SEA SPARKLE

NOTES USED - G, A, B, C, D, E, F

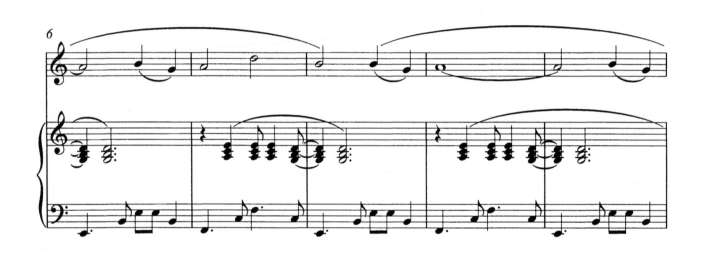

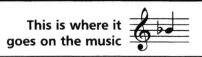

This is where it goes on the music

To play B♭ press the keys coloured black

Left hand

Right hand

MORNING IN MOSCOW

NOTES USED - G, A, C, E, low D, F, B♭

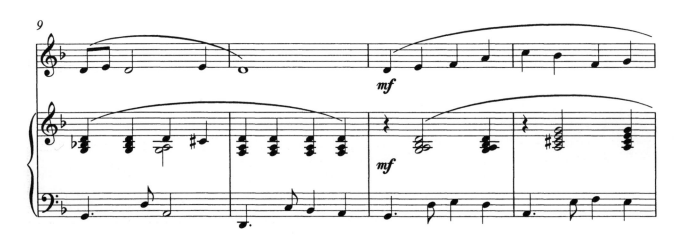

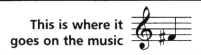

and finally F#

This is where it goes on the music

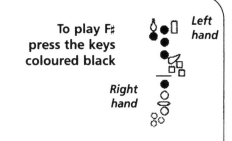

To play F#
press the keys
coloured black

Left hand

Right hand

SHRIMP SHUFFLE

NOTES USED - G, A, B, C, D, E, low D, F, B♭, F#

Cool and laid back (♩ = 110)

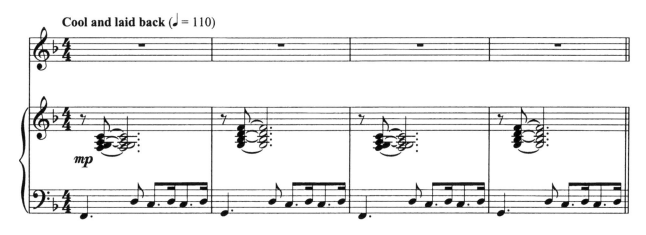

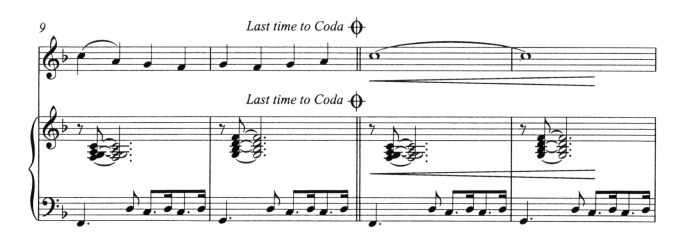

© Copyright 2003 Kevin Mayhew Ltd.
It is illegal to photocopy music.

27

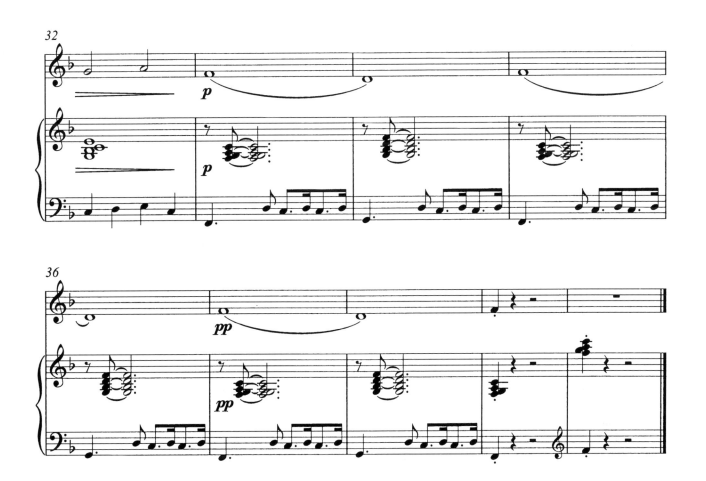

BANANA TANGO

NOTES USED - G, A, B, C, D, E, F, F♯

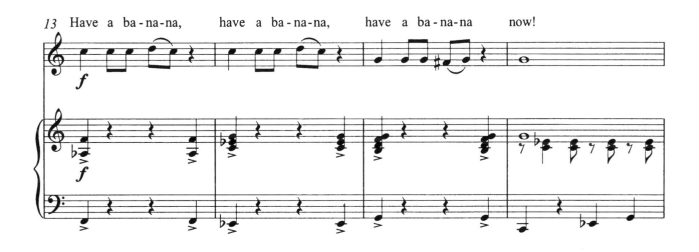

Have a ba-na-na, have a ba-na-na, have a ba-na-na now!

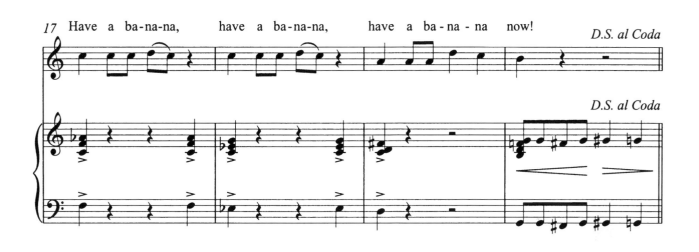

Have a ba-na-na, have a ba-na-na, have a ba-na-na now!

D.S. al Coda

D.S. al Coda

CODA

Have a ba-na-na now!

CODA

Have a ba-na-na now!

31